CW00035747

Holmes, Chemistry and the Royal Institution

Holmes, Chemistry and the Royal Institution

Antony J. Richards & Bryson Gore

Edited by Antony J. Richards

Holmes, Chemistry and the Royal Institution

Antony J. Richards, M.R.I. & Bryson Gore, M.A.

Edited by Antony J. Richards, M.R.I.

First Published in 1998
Printed by E. & E. Plumridge Ltd., 41 High Street, Linton,
Cambridge CB1 6HS.

ISBN: 1-901091-01-5

Produced in conjunction with the Sherlock Holmes
Society of London
© A. J. Richards and B. Gore, 1998
All rights in individual contributions are retained by the
authors.

Typeset in Baskerville

Cover: Sherlock Holmes, with Dr. Watson in attendance,
delivering one of the Friday evening discourses at the Royal
Institution of Great Britain, as captured by Douglas E.
West.

Inside front cover: Faraday delivering his Christmas Lecture,
1856, with The Prince Consort and The Prince of Wales in
attendance. (Reproduced courtesy of the Library and
Information Centre, Royal Society of Chemistry

Contents

Foreword

Doctor Antony J. Richards, M.R.I.

It was on the evening of Thursday, 27th. October, 1994 that members of the Sherlock Holmes Society of London made a journey, not two miles distant from Baker Street, to Albemarle Street in the West End of London where may be found the home of the Royal Institution of Great Britain. The Royal Institution of Great Britain has been justifiably depicted as the cradle of British science ever since it was founded by Count Rumford in 1799. Since then it has welcomed through its doors scholars, philosophers, scientists, artists and laymen from all walks of life with the common aim of furthering their scientific knowledge. It was once said by a speaker at the Royal Institution of Great Britain that, of all places on Earth, the Institution has seen the greatest number of discoveries per square metre. This assertion has not been challenged to date. Best known of the Directors and occupants of the 21 Albemarle Street residence was Michael Faraday, the 'father of electricity', who resided in the building for some fifty years and was responsible for the discovery of electromagnetic induction and many of the laws of physics and chemistry which have shaped the modern world.

Hence it was entirely appropriate that the Sherlock Holmes Society of London should choose this illustrious and historic venue for a discourse delivered by Dr. Bryson Gore entitled 'Chemistry is ...... Elementary'. Dr. Gore has had a long association with the Royal Institution of Great Britain, having been the 'Clothworkers' Lecturer and Lecturers' Superintendent', the equivalent post once occupied by Faraday shortly after he entered the Institution on 1st. March, 1813. Undoubtedly, the place had already enjoyed a golden age during the period when Holmes was most active, although the institution was still just as popular under the new directorships of John Tyndall, Sir James Dewar, Lord Rayleigh and Sir William Bragg. It must come as a surprise then that there is no mention by Watson of Holmes, a more than competent experimental chemist in his own right, ever having attended a discourse in this building. The discourses, which take place twenty times a year on Friday evenings between the lecture theatre clock chiming nine and ten o'clock, must have had scientific appeal to Holmes. Indeed, Appendix A lists some of the discourses which may have been of interest to Holmes, as well as those which a certain professor of mathematics might have attended.

There is evidence to suggest that Holmes may have led a double life for it is well known that a Professor Holmes did do research in collaboration with Faraday on none other than an electric generator for providing an arc lamp for lighthouses (although there are no records indicating the presence of a trained cormorant involved with this research!). However, this link is not to be for Faraday died in 1867 when Holmes was a mere teenager, and before Holmes came to London, so it is improbable that these two great figures ever met. This does not, of course, preclude Professor Holmes being the father of Sherlock

Holmes and an inspiration for the latter's scientific knowledge.

What follows is a short introduction to the history of the Royal Institution of Great Britain, a review of the chemical references in the cases of Sherlock Holmes, an illustrated transcript of the discourse given by Dr. Bryson Gore on Thursday 27th. October, 1994, a look at the similarity in characters between Faraday and Holmes and, finally, the exposition of a theory which links Holmes to the Royal Institution of Great Britain and also provides some new light on one of the most famous unchronicled cases of Sherlock Holmes.

It is sincerely hoped that the reader will agree with the words used by Ben Jonson, in connection with Shakespeare, and apply them equally to Sherlock Holmes, Michael Faraday and the Royal Institution of Great Britain − "He was not of an age, but for all time"!

Acknowledgements

Doctor Antony J. Richards, M.R.I.
Doctor Bryson Gore, M.A.

Unlike Mr. Sherlock Holmes who "though he docketed any fresh information very quickly and accurately in his brain, he seldom made any acknowledgement to the giver" the authors of this publication should like to thank all those who have contributed to 'Holmes, Chemisty & the Royal Institution'.

Most notable among these are M. C. Black, Catherine Cooke, Derek Hinrich, Julie Mellowes and Doctor Gavin Squire for their generous support in proof reading the text before publication. Lesley Freeman is acknowledged for having completed the unenviable task of audio-typing the original discourse complete with sound effects.

Help with some of the historical researches and illustrations was given by Irena McCabe, the Librarian at the Royal Institution of Great Britain and Nicola Best, the Senior Library Assistant at the Royal Society of Chemistry.

The authors would also like to acknowledge Trinity House and the National Trust for their help in connection with information on the South Foreland lighthouse.

The Royal Institution Of Great Britain: Place of Tradition and Chemical Genius

Doctor Antony J. Richards, M.R.I.

"A loyalist, traitor, spy, cryptographer, opportunist, womaniser, philanthropist, egotistical bore, soldier of fortune, military and technical advisor, inventor, plagiarist ..." This is not the cast list from one of Dr. Watson's writings, but the description given by W. H. Brock in *New Scientist* (27th. March, 1980) of one man, Sir Benjamin Thompson otherwise known as Count Rumford (**Figure 1**), who was also an "... expert on heat (especially fireplaces and ovens) and founder of the world's greatest showplace for the popularisation of science, the Royal Institution".

The Institution may never have been founded if this American-born scientist and statesman had not been accused of spying and fled from his native land to London where he acquired British citizenship. In time he became head of the military forces of Bavaria and 'Envoy Extraordinary to the Court of St. James'. However, George III refused to accept one of his own subjects as a foreign minister. It was now that Rumford, with the support of Sir Joseph Banks, the President of the Royal Society, founded the Royal Institution of Great Britain (**Figure 2**) in 1799.

Figure 1 — Benjamin Thompson, later known as Count Rumford, founder of the Royal Institution of Great Britain. (*The Story of Nineteenth Century Science,* Henry Smith Williams, M.D., Harper and Brothers Publishers, London & New York, 1900)

Figure 2 Façade of the Royal Institution of Great Britain. (*Old and New London: A Narrative of its History, its People, and its Places*, Volume IV, Edward Walford, Cassell Peter & Galpin, London, Paris & New York, 1893)

THE ROYAL INSTITUTION OF GREAT BRITAIN

3

Rumford was destined not to see the full fruits of his labour, for three years later, he had a disagreement with the managers of the Royal Institution of Great Britain and consequently left London in favour of France and Anne Lavoisier, the widow of the chemist Antoine Lavoisier, whom he was to marry. He never returned to London.

The Institution which he founded was a great success from the outset. People flocked to the lectures and exhibitions held there. Maybe the best service Rumford did the Royal Institution of Great Britain was in 1802 when he recruited Thomas Young **(Figure 3)** and Humphry Davy **(Figure 4)**. Both were exceptional scientists, but Davy had an extra quality. Young was appointed as 'Professor of Natural Philosophy' and during his time at the Institution was to resurrect the wave theory of light with his famous fringe experiment, decipher part of the Rosetta stone, design many optical instruments as well as write papers on a wide variety of subjects such as the theory of capillarity and surfaces.

Despite all of these achievements, it was the Cornishman who had been appointed 'Assistant Lecturer' who is among the names best associated with the Royal Institution of Great Britain. Unfortunately, it became clear that Young as a lecturer was a failure, while Davy on the other hand was a brilliant orator. He would keep the attention of his audience with his fluent delivery and breath-taking demonstrations. Indeed Coleridge once said that he went to the institution "to renew my stock of metaphors". He also said that had Davy not "been the first chemist, he would have been the first poet of the

Figure 3 — Thomas Young famous for his researches into the wave theory of light and for deciphering part of the Rosetta stone. (Reproduced in *The Story of Nineteenth Century Science*, Henry Smith Williams, M.D., Harper and Brothers Publishers, London & New York, 1900)

Figure 4 – Sir Humphry Davy, scientist, poet and 'Director' of the Royal Institution of Great Britain. (*The Story of Nineteenth Century Science,* Henry Smith Williams, M.D., Harper and Brothers Publishers, London & New York, 1900)

age". The Institution soon became an important social venue which undoubtedly added to its prestige at this time.

These poetic descriptions of Davy should in no way detract from the scientific achievements of the man which were immense. While at the Royal Institution of Great Britain he was to discover sodium, potassium, calcium, barium, strontium and magnesium. He isolated boron and clarified the nature of iodine. Davy also established a laboratory (**Figure 5**) in the basement, now called the 'Davy Faraday Laboratory', which was acclaimed to be one of the finest and best equipped in the world. It predates the 'Clarendon' in Oxford, and the 'Cavendish' in Cambridge, by some sixty years.

If that were not enough, he invented the electric arc, the miners' safety lamp which bears his name, methods for bleaching cloth, copying paintings on ceramics, tanning leather, and arresting the corrosion of ships as well as other contributions to our knowledge of geology, mineralogy and agricultural chemistry. Davy was also a founding member of the Athenaeum Club, London Zoo, the London Zoological Society and the Geological Society. Socially he mixed with the likes of Wordsworth, Byron, Coleridge, Southey and Walter Scott. In 1802 he became 'Professor of Chemistry', in 1804 'Director' and thereafter he held the post of 'Honorary Professor' until his death in 1829. However, it was said by Davy himself that his greatest discovery of all was Michael Faraday (**Figure 6**), a man who was to put even Davy's achievements in the shade.

Figure 5 – Michael Faraday behind the chemical bench in the basement laboratory of the Royal Institution of Great Britain which was originally established by Sir Humphry Davy. *(Famous Chemists: The Men and their Work,* Sir William A. Tilden, F.R.S., D.Sc., LL.D., Sc.D., George Routledge & Sons,Ltd., New York, 1921)

Figure 6 — Michael Faraday, Sir Humphry Davy's most important discovery. (*Famous Chemists: The Men and their Work,* Sir William A. Tilden, F.R.S., D.Sc., LL.D., Sc.D., George Routledge & Sons, Ltd., New York, 1921)

Faraday had no formal education, but what he lacked in knowledge he made up for in enthusiasm. In 1812 a Mr. Charles' Dance, a customer of the bookbinder to whom Faraday was apprenticed, gave Faraday a ticket to attend a lecture at the Institution to be delivered by Davy. He took copious amounts of notes which he later rewrote, adding illustrations, and bound. These he sent to Davy asking for a job. Davy interviewed Faraday early in 1813 but, although impressed with him, there was alas no vacancy. However, as fate would have it, shortly afterwards an assistant in the laboratory was dismissed for brawling and Faraday was taken on from 1st. March, 1813, at a salary of twenty-five shillings a week, with two rooms at the top of the building.

Faraday had a natural talent for the job and within days became a most able assistant to Davy in his researches. This is where he learnt his experimental skills. In the autumn of 1813, despite England being at war with France, Davy was to embark on a scientific tour of Europe to last eighteen months. This tour was made possible only by the great regard Napoleon had for science in general and Davy in particular, who had in 1808 received the Napoleon prize of three thousand francs for his electrical researches. Faraday went along as his secretary and scientific assistant. It was during this tour that Faraday was to complete his scientific education by meeting some of the greatest scientists in the world at that, or any other, time. These included Ampère, Gay-Lussac, Arago, Humboldt, Cuvier, Rumford and Volta.

10

On his return to London, Faraday was made 'Assistant in the Laboratory and Mineralogical Collection and Superintendent of the Apparatus'. His salary was also increased to one hundred pounds per annum at which it stayed until 1853. It was soon apparent that Faraday as a lecturer surpassed even Davy, and the same was true of his researches. In 1825 Faraday was made 'Director of the Laboratory' and in 1826 he inaugurated the Christmas lectures for children **(Figure 7)**. He held many appointments, including membership of the 'Senate of the University of London'. He was a 'Scientific Advisor' to Trinity House, and to the 'Scientific Advising Committee to the Admiralty', a lecturer in chemistry at the 'Royal Military Academy' in Woolwich and held numerous consultancies all of which could have made him a rich man.

Faraday's scientific work was certainly varied, there being over sixteen thousand entries in his laboratory notebooks between 1831 and 1860. He is best known, though, for his work on the relationship between electricity and magnetism, the propagation of electrical and magnetic effects, electricity and matter, light and electromagnetism and the underlying unity of physical phenomena. This included work on the miners' safety lamp, the preparation of alloy steels, the discovery of benzene, researches on the vulcanisation of rubber, various photochemical preparations, the production of optical grade glass, the liquefaction of gases including chlorine, defining the laws of electrolysis, the discovery of superionic conductors, the catalytic action of platinum, selective adsorption of ethene and carbon dioxide, magneto-chemistry and the magnetic

Figure 7 — Michael Faraday lecturing to children at the Royal Institution of Great Britain. (Reproduced Courtesy of the Library & Information Centre, Royal Society of Chemistry)

properties of matter, the 'Faraday effect' (i.e. the rotation of the plane of polarisation of light by a magnetic field), electromagnetic rotations which led to the first electric motor, electromagnetic induction, electrostatics, the 'Faraday cage' (which demonstrated that charge resides on the surface of a conductor and not within), the 'Faraday dark space' (which related how the various forms of electric discharge between conductors in an evacuated enclosure, in particular the 'dark' discharge near the cathode, changed as the pressure of the residual gas decreased) and the relationship between light, electricity and magnetism.

It is no wonder that he suffered a complete breakdown of health in 1840 and was forced to rest completely for a year. It is true to say that after this date he continued to do brilliant work but that it had to be interspersed with periods for rest and recovery. He gave his last Christmas lecture in 1860, and performed his final experiments and gave his last discourse in 1862. He resigned all duties in 1865, and died peacefully on 25th. August 1867 at Hampton Court **(Figure 8)** where, at Prince Albert's suggestion, the Queen had given Faraday a 'Grace and Favour Residence'.

Upon retirement in 1865 Faraday had handed over his office to John Tyndall **(Figure 9)**, an Irishman, who had been appointed 'Professor of Natural Philosophy' in 1853 and had become a firm friend and colleague of Faraday. He maintained the best traditions of the Institution as a place for pioneering research. He explained the flow of glaciers, was the first to measure the absorption and

Figure 8 – Michael Faraday's home at Hampton Court (*Michael Faraday: His Life and Work*, Silvanus P. Thompson, D.Sc., F.R.S., Cassell and Company, Ltd., London, Paris, New York & Melbourne, 1898)

Figure 9 — An 1868 photograph of John Tyndall by Sawyer of Norwich. (*Life and Work of John Tyndall,* Professor A. S. Eve, F.R.S. and C. H. Creasey, O.B.E., Macmillan & Co. Ltd., London, 1945)

radiation of heat by gases and vapours, identified what has become known as the 'greenhouse effect', explained the scattering of light by small particles, which to this day is called the Tyndall effect, and participated in bacteriological work in conjunction with the botanical gardens at Kew. He was also a great showman which led to his discourses being a great success.

In 1887 James Dewar (**Figure 10**) became 'Fullerian Professor of Chemistry'. He was an ideal candidate to carry on the traditions of the Institution being a great chemist, brilliant experimentalist, accomplished musician, keen astronomer and lover of poetry. He overlapped with Tyndall for ten years, but unfortunately in the latter years the two great men had a strained relationship. This came to a head when in 1887 the managers of the Institution decided that the Christmas lectures for that year, which were to be given by an ageing Tyndall, should instead be delivered by Dewar. Tyndall took this personally and resigned, with the consequence that Dewar became the 'Superintendent of the House'. However, this did not affect the prestige of the place, and the discourses were as popular as ever with poets, musicians, actors, artists and leading scientists of the day being among those asked to give lectures. These included Sir Henry Irving, Pierre Curie, Alfred Wallace and Nikola Tesla.

The successor to Tyndall as 'Professor of Natural Philosophy' was John William Strutt, who was later to become Lord Rayleigh (**Figure 11**). He was an eminent Cambridge scientist who, in 1879, was appointed

Figure 10 — James Dewar, chemist, experimentalist, musician, astronomer and poet. (*British Chemists*, Edited by Alexander Findlay and William Hobson Mills, London Chemical Society, 1946)

Figure 11 – Lord Rayleigh, the Essex farmer, who became 'Cavendish Professor of Physics' in 1879. (Reproduced Courtesy of the Library & Information Centre, Royal Society of Chemistry)

'Cavendish Professor of Physics' following the death of Clerk Maxwell, but he was also a gentleman farmer and resigned the position in 1884 in order to attend to his estate at Terling in Essex. He set up a private laboratory in his house and continued researches here and at the Institution until 1905. During this time he explained the 'blue sky effect', pioneered studies in sound and surface acoustical waves, optics, fluid mechanics and colloid science. He was awarded the Nobel prize in 1904 for the discovery of argon. He was also extremely well connected for his brother-in-law was no other than Balfour, who became Prime Minister and later Foreign Secretary. The latter attended the Friday evening discourses on numerous occasions, and no doubt this had an effect upon the Government's view on the importance of science.

Among other important events at the Royal Institution of Great Britain was the announcement of the discovery of the electron by J. J. Thomson, Rayleigh's successor as 'Cavendish Professor of Physics' at Cambridge, in 1897. In 1926 Logie Baird gave the first demonstration of television, while in 1931 Maynard Keynes described 'The Internal Mechanics of the Trade Slump'. The Institution was also the place where, in 1932, Lord Rutherford announced the discovery of the neutron. Another landmark was the finding by W. H. Bragg that hair, wool and other natural fibres are, in fact, crystalline. This marked the beginning of structural molecular biology. A more recent discourse concerned the Nobel-prize-winning research which elucidated the structure of haemoglobin and myoglobin (Max Perutz and John Kendrew).

Meanwhile, in 1965, David Phillips, working in the 'Davy Faraday Laboratory', produced a world first by solving the structure of lysozyme. To date, fifteen professors of the Royal Institution of Great Britain have been Nobel laureates.

This is just a short potted history of the people who have made the Royal Institution of Great Britain **the** place for science and education. To do full justice to the achievements and personalities involved would take many volumes, but the reader should be aware that it is a place which is seldom equalled and never surpassed, and for this reason alone it seems to this author inconceivable that somebody as competent a scientist as Mr. Sherlock Holmes did not, at sometime, either attend discourses, or conduct researches, or deliver a discourse, at this fashionable address so close to those famous rooms at 221B Baker Street.

Bibliography

The House of the Royal Institution, A. D. R. Caroe, Oliver Burridge & Co. (1963).

Michael Faraday and the Modern World, Brian Bowers, EPA Press (1991).

Michael Faraday and the Royal Institution (The Genius of Man and Place), John Meurig Thomas, IOP Publishing (1991).

Michael Faraday of the Royal Institution, Ronald King, The Royal Institution of Great Britain (1973).

Sherlock Holmes: A Study In Chemistry

Doctor Antony J. Richards, M.R.I.

Holmes' scientific knowledge, according to Watson's report on Holmes in *A Study in Scarlet,* was non-uniform. Of astronomy Holmes was marked as having no knowledge, and although his anatomy knowledge was accurate it was unsystematic. Holmes faired better in botany where he was well up on belladonna, opium and poisons in general. Knowledge of geology was practical but limited since it was mainly confined to the identification of soil types. However, when it came to chemistry, Watson could only say that Holmes' knowledge was "profound". Watson later added to this assertion in *The Five Orange Pips* by saying that Holmes' chemistry was "eccentric".

Despite this, Watson certainly regarded his friend as a chemist and said as much in *The Valley of Fear* when, describing Holmes' face on hearing of the death of John Douglas, he wrote: "There was no trace of the horror which I had myself felt at this curt declaration, but his face showed rather the quiet and interested composure of the chemist who sees the crystals falling into position from his over-saturated solution". It could also be said that Holmes' entire method of deductive reasoning is akin to that required by an analytical chemist of the first order.

23

The visible evidence also pointed to Holmes being a chemist. Watson, describing Holmes in *A Study in Scarlet*, says that his hands were "invariably blotted with ink and stained with chemicals". He had noted this feature earlier, in the same narrative, while Holmes was placing a plaster on his finger at St. Bartholomew's Hospital his hand: "was mottled over with similar pieces of plaster, and discoloured with strong acids".

It would appear that chemistry was as much a part of Holmes' life as the cocaine he frequently took. Watson writes, in *The Three Students*, that "My friend's temper had not been improved since he had been deprived of the congenial surroundings of Baker Street. Without his scrap-books, his chemicals, and his homely untidiness, he was an uncomfortable man". Holmes was certainly a practicing chemist since Watson often complained about Holmes's experiments, noting in *The Musgrave Ritual* that "Our chambers were always full of chemicals and of criminal relics, which had a way of wandering into unlikely positions, and of turning up in the butter-dish, or in even less desirable places".

Often the experiments could not have endeared themselves to Mrs. Hudson, or for that matter Watson, since in *The Dancing Men* it is stated that "Holmes had been seated for some hours in silence, with his long, thin back curved over a chemical vessel in which he was brewing a particularly malodorous product". This very point is made again in *The Sign of Four* in which Watson wrote: "He would hardly reply to my questions, and busied himself all the evening in an abstruce chemical analysis which involved much heating of retorts and distilling of vapours, ending at last in a smell which fairly drove me out of the apartment".

The experiments were conducted in a corner of the Baker Street rooms which was specially set aside for this purpose. This is mentioned in *The Empty House* where Watson informs the reader that "There were the chemical corner and the acid-stained deal-topped table" and also in *The Mazarin Stone* where "He looked round him at the scientific charts upon the wall, the acid-charred bench of chemicals, the violin-case leaning in the corner, the coal-scuttle, which contained of old pipes and tobacco". Certainly one of the best known illustrations **(Figure 1)** was done by Sidney Paget for *The Naval Treaty* in which Holmes is shown pursuing his chemical experiments. The laboratory was, by all accounts, well equipped with apparatus for there is mention of Bunsen burners, litmus paper, pipettes, retorts and a microscope being present. Among the chemicals most used by Holmes were acetones, acids such as hydrochloric (and also prussic as sent to Holmes by Eugenia Ronder in *The Veiled Lodger*), alkalis such as baryta, other inorganics like bisulphate of baryta, and various hydrocarbons.

However, Holmes was interested in chemistry long before taking up residence in Baker Street, since he mentions in *The Gloria Scott* that during his college days in one of the long vacations after returning from Donnithorpe, where his friend Victor Trevor lived, he "went up to my London rooms, where I spent seven weeks working out a few experiments in organic chemistry".

Figure 1 — Holmes the chemist as illustrated by Sidney Paget for *The Naval Treaty*. This case was first published in two parts during October and November, 1893.

The chemical pursuits, though, were erratic in nature and liable to be done at any time of day or night as illustrated in *The Copper Beeches* when a telegram arrives for Holmes just when Watson "was thinking of turning in, and Holmes was settling down to one of those all-night researches which he frequently indulged in, when I would leave him stooping over a retort and a test-tube at night, and find him in the same position when I came down to breakfast in the morning". The same point is made in *The Sign of Four* in which Watson states that "Up to the small hours of the morning I could hear the clinking of his test-tubes, which told me that he was still engaged in his malodorous experiment".

So, what of the chemical researches themselves? Most are mentioned in passing but three may be considered to be of true significance. The first takes place at St. Bartholomew's Hospital where Holmes and Watson meet for the first time in *A Study in Scarlet*. Indeed the first sighting of Holmes by Watson was him "bending over a distant table absorbed in his work" in "a lofty chamber, lined and littered with countless bottles" where "Broad, low tables were scattered about, which bristled with retorts, test-tubes, and little Bunsen lamps, with their blue flickering flames". Further, the very first words Holmes speaks are:

> "'I've found it! I've found it,' he shouted to my companion, running towards us with a test-tube in his hand **(Figure 2)**. 'I have found a reagent which is precipitated by haemoglobin, and by nothing else'".

27

Figure 2 — The first meeting of Holmes and Watson in a chemical laboratory at St. Batholomew's Hospital in *A Study in Scarlet*. The illustrator was George Hutchinson who viewed Holmes a little differently from the later, and better known, drawings of Sidney Paget (**Figures 1 & 3**).

What Holmes had found was "the most practical medico-legal discovery for years". Indeed it was "an infallible test for blood stains". Holmes continued his explanation saying that:

> "The old guaiacum test was very clumsy and uncertain. So is the microscopic examination for blood corpuscles. The latter is valueless if the stains are a few hours old. Now, this appears to act as well whether the blood is old or new. Had this test been invented, there are hundreds of men now walking the earth who would long ago have paid the penalty of their crimes."

It is interesting to note here that shortly afterwards, while Holmes is describing his habits to Watson prior to their taking rooms at Baker Street, Holmes states that "I generally have chemicals about, and occasionally do experiments". In light of what has already been written, the former statement would seem to be accurate while the latter may lack some veracity. This is probably due to the fact that Holmes did not wish to put off his prospective flat companion from agreeing to share diggings, especially since Stamford states that Holmes "was complaining that you could get no one to go halves with you".

The second experiment of note takes place in *A Case of Identity*. Watson had been out all day on "A professional case of great gravity" and returns to Baker Street to find Holmes "half asleep, with his long, thin form curled up in the recesses of his arm-chair. A formidable array of bottles and test-tubes, with the pungent cleanly smell of hydrochloric acid, told me that he had spent his day in the chemical work which was so dear to him" **(Figure 3)**. Watson asks if Holmes had solved the case of Miss Sutherland, to which Holmes, thinking that Watson is referring to his chemical work, replies that it was bisulphate of baryta. As to the significance of the work, the reader is not informed, but it can be inferred that this result helped bring another criminal to justice.

Holmes' chemistry is again in action, this time with a life or death consequence, in *The Naval Treaty*. Watson describes the event perfectly:

> "Holmes was seated at his side-table clad in his dressing-gown and working hard over a chemical investigation. A large curved retort was boiling furiously in the bluish flame of a Bunsen burner, and the distilled drops were condensing into a two-litre measure. My friend hardly glanced up as I entered, and I, seeing that his investigation must be of importance, seated myself in an arm-chair and waited. He dipped into this bottle or that, drawing out a few drops of each with his glass pipette, and finally brought a test-tube containing a solution over to the table. In his right hand he had a slip of litmus-paper.
>
> 'You come at a crisis, Watson,' said he. 'If this paper remains blue, all is well. If it turns red, it means a man's life.' He dipped it into the test-tube, and it flushed at once into a dull, dirty crimson. 'Hum! I thought as much!' he cried. 'I

Figure 3 – Holmes as seen through the eyes of Sidney Paget from *A Case of Identity*, first published in September, 1891.

shall be at your service in one instant, Watson. You will find tobacco in the Persian slipper.' He turned to his desk and scribbled off several telegrams, which were handed over to the pageboy. Then he threw himself down in the chair opposite, and drew up his knees until his fingers clasped round his long, thin shins.

'A very commonplace little murder,' said he".

There are other mentions of chemical experiments. For instance, during the 'Great Hiatus', Holmes "spent some months in a research into coal-tar derivatives, which I conducted in a laboratory at Montpelier, in the south of France" as revealed in *The Empty House*.

Again, in *A Study in Scarlet* Holmes, by way of relaxation, plunges into a chemical analysis. In *The Resident Patient* there is mention of a chemical experiment though this reference was omitted from the 1928 omnibus volume and all subsequent editions of that case. In *The Devil's Foot* Holmes performs what might be termed a chemical experiment to see what affect heating the *radix pedis diaboli* has on himself and Watson. This had near fatal results though it did help prove who the murderer was in that instance. Holmes examined some threads under a microscope in order to identify some blobs of glue in *The Adventure of Shoscombe Old Place* and hence confirmed that the owner of the cap found beside the dead policeman in the St. Pancras case was the picture-frame maker who had been accused of the crime. In the same narrative Holmes refers to another microscopy examination he had previously performed in which he identified zinc and copper filings in the seam of a cuff of a coiner.

Of course, one of the major functions of a practising chemist is to publish results for the furtherance of science. Holmes was active in this respect by being the author of several monographs on chemical matters. The most famous is probably "Upon the Distinction Between the Ashes of the Various Tobaccos" mentioned in *A Study in Scarlet, The Boscombe Valley Mystery* and *The Sign of Four*. Others such as those on ciphers, the dating of documents, the tracing of footprints, the form of the hand in relation to trade, the uses of dogs in the work of the detective, the typewriter and its relation to crime and the "Practical Handbook of Bee Culture" may, or may not, have had chemical content, though each in their own right would have been of interest scientifically.

In conclusion, for Holmes chemistry was not just one facet of his detective work, but was a passion in itself. By the time of *The Final Problem* Holmes indicates that, should he free the world of Moriarty, he would be happy to live a more "placid line of life" in which he "could continue to live in the quiet fashion which is most congenial to me, and to concentrate my attention upon my chemical researches". In the same case Holmes told Watson that "Of late I have been tempted to look into the problems furnished by nature rather than those more superficial ones for which our artificial state of society is responsible". It can only be assumed that this is indeed what Holmes did in retirement and that somewhere along the south coast of England there is a small cottage with a beekeeper and a corner of a room set aside for chemical researches.

Bibliography

The Complete Sherlock Holmes, Sir Arthur Conan Doyle, Blitz Editions (undated).

The Encyclopaedia Sherlockiana, Jack Tracy, Avenue Books (1987).

The Sherlock Holmes Encyclopaedia, Matthew E. Bunson, Pavilion Books (1995).

Further Reading

Chemistry and Crime: From Sherlock Holmes to Today's Courtroom, Edited by Samuel M. Gerber, American Chemical Society, Washington, D.C. (1983).

The Modern Sherlock Holmes: An Introduction to Forensic Science Today, Judy Williams, Broadside Books Ltd., London (1991).

Chemistry is ...... Elementary

Doctor Bryson Gore, M.A.

The story that I have to tell you is a detective story. In fact it's a chemical detective story. It is a true story although I have to admit there are certain elements in it that have been embellished for the sake of entertainment, but I will leave it to your own analysis as to which parts are true and which are embellishment. The story recounts mankind's search for the elements of life, the chemical constituents of nature, and I think it is appropriate that the story is one of the application of observation, analysis and deduction.

Science, by observing nature and analysing the results, has been able to deduce nature's composition. The bulk of our story takes place in the nineteenth century when the research that forms the basis of our current knowledge of the elements was performed, but in truth it starts much much longer ago than that. I think we all know that the ancients believed that the universe seemed to be made from simpler elements, namely earth, air, fire and water, but as we look at that idea and as we continue through our subject I would hope that you will remember that not everything is quite as it seems and very little of it is simple.

Let us think of those four elements. We know that if we strike a match in air we can create a flame and that the air will support the flame. But if we collect the air produced from fermenting grapes to form wine, trap it in a glass vessel and we place our match within that air, it will not support combustion and the flame is extinguished. On

35

the other hand, if we disturb the rotting vegetation at the bottom of a lake or stagnant pond, as I am sure Holmes did in his youth and as I am sure that many in the past would have done, we can collect a different gas, another air so to speak. If again we take our lighted match and place it within the glass vessel ......

BANG !!!

...... the result is altogether more vigorous and shocking. Not all air is the same and much the same is true of water. Water we are all familiar with, water is all around us. I can take a glass of water and we are all familiar with its behaviour but sometimes ......

WHOOSH !!!

...... a glass of *water* (liquid nitrogen), by simple contact with the ground, will instantly return to air. So, not all water is water and even with the most familiar of facts, i.e. that water will extinguish a fire, we find that we can no longer be so sure. I have here a glass of water, I can drink it to quench my thirst. In front of me I have an intimate mixture of a fuel and a source of oxygen but no reaction is taking place. I take a few drops of water from my glass and add it to the mixture ......

BANG!!!
...... I can use water not only to extinguish a fire but also to create

one. As I stated in my introduction, not everything is as it seems and very little is simple.

But let us go back and actually think briefly about the ancient Greeks and the concept of elements. It is often said that, in order to answer the question "What is the universe made from?", the Greeks invented the concept of the four elements. I wish to state that this assertion is doubly false! Firstly, I am certain that many people, prior to the ancient Greeks, had proposed that the four elements were central to an understanding of nature. The Greeks, however, were the first people who wrote it down, the books survived to be rediscovered during the Renaissance and that is why we give them the credit. But, secondly, I would like you to think about a Greek philosopher, two thousand years ago after a hard day at work, going down to the beach to sit outside a taverna, sipping a beaker of wine and contemplating nature.

If a philosopher, in that situation, had asked himself, or herself, "What is the universe made from?", "What is the world around me made from?", it is not entirely surprising that they should conclude that the earth upon which they sat, the air that they breathed, the water of the Aegean lapping gently on the shores of the beach and that the fire that cooked their supper were all constituents.

But it has always struck me that to stop at that conclusion is an example of 'the curious incident of the dog in the night-time'. Because Holmes was right to point out that the curious incident was that the dog did nothing in the night. If you were sitting on that beach contemplating what the universe was made from it strikes me that there is one significant omission from that list. Surely, if you were analysing the universe you would have earth, air, fire, water and life. Life is not on that list, and I believe it is not there because that was not the question that the Greek philosopher was asking. The question was not "What is the universe made from?" but a simpler, much more directly relevant one, "What am I made from?" This was a difficult question to answer because the ancient Greeks didn't know where babies came from; well − in one sense they did, but they did not know how a living being was created. The concept of the four elements comes from a brilliant piece of scientific deduction: the ancients did not know where life came from but they did know where life went. After a death what methods did they have for disposing of a body? They could carry it to the top of a hill, leave it there for a few weeks and when they came back it had gone, vanished into thin air. They could dig a hole and put it in the ground, and should they be so macabre as to dig it up at a later time, it would have gone, turned into earth. They could sail out to sea and drop the body overboard and it was gone, turned into water. Or, finally, they could build a fire, put the body on top and burn it and see it turn into fire. These were the four destinations of life and, as such, if life could be converted into those four 'elements' then surely it is made from them?

So, by two thousand years ago philosophers had established, by the application of scientific deduction, that life and everything else in the universe was formed from earth, air, fire and water, and that philosophy held sway for thousands of years because later philosophers were generally in awe of the ancient Greeks.

Our story now jumps to a point just two hundred years ago. I wish to quote to you from a book written in 1803 by a Mrs. Marcet (**Figure 1**). She was not a chemist by training and in the introduction to her book entitled *Conversations in Chemistry*, she apologised to her audience for the fact that she was not a chemist but had only learnt her subject in recent months and, at this point, I should make a similar admission. I am a physicist both by nature and training and, as such, much of what I have said and will go on to say, would not be considered to be strictly main-stream chemistry.

Mrs. Marcet's book took the form of a series of conversations between a Mrs. B (why Mrs. Marcet should have labelled herself as Mrs. B I have never understood) and a number of young women. The book was written in 1803 and even then we find on page 9,

Caroline

But do not fire, air, earth and water, consist, each of them, but of one kind of substance?

Mrs. B.

No, my dear; they are every one of them

Figure 1 — Mrs. Jane Marcet, the author of
Conversations in Chemistry. (*Old
Chemistries*, Edgar F. Smith, McGraw-Hill
Book Company, Inc., New York, 1927)

susceptible of being separated into various simple bodies. Instead of four, chemists now reckon upwards of forty elementary substances. These we shall examine separately, and afterwards consider in their combinations with each other.

Their names are as follows:

Light	Silex	Zinc
Caloric	Alumine	Bismuth
Oxygen	Yttria	Antimony
Nitrogen	Glucina	Arsenic
Hydrogen	Zirconia	Cobalt
Sulphur	Agustina	Manganese
Phosphorus	(25 metals.)	Tungsten
Carbone	Gold	Molybdenum
(2 Alkalies.)	Platina	Uranium
Potash	Silver	Tellurium
Soda	Mercury	Titanium
(10 Earths.)	Copper	Chrome
Lime	Iron	Osmium
Magnesia	Tin	Iridium
Strontites	Lead	Palladium
Barytes	Nickel	Rhodium

Let us consider the substances that Mrs. Marcet believed to be elements, just 200 years ago. Light and caloric (caloric, for those of you who are unaware, is the old name for heat); neither is nowadays considered to be a chemical element, but oxygen, nitrogen, hydrogen, sulphur, phosphorus, carbon (although spelt somewhat oddly) are entirely correct. Then comes a whole list of total mistakes. Potash, soda, lime, magnesia, silex, alumine, yttria, glucina, zirconia, and agustina. Not only are none of those elements, but in fact austina contains the same basic element as lime and in an edition of this book that appeared a few years later agustina had disappeared from the list. Each of these 'elements' is composed of a variety of elements. Then comes another good long run of true elements from gold to rhodium, including uranium. I have to say that I was really surprised to learn that they were aware that uranium was an element two hundred years ago. I can only surmise that uranium ore deposits were discovered very early, and that holds the key to what we will shortly discover about the nineteenth century analytical chemist. So, these were the elements two hundred years ago with, as I say, a slight error in the central section.

How had scientists derived this list and how did they analyse the substances that were around them to determine the elements of which they were composed? Well, this was really the fundamental role of the nineteenth century chemist. It strikes me that when we think of a modern chemist, we think of somebody synthesising chemicals, that is, making new chemicals. This is a fundamentally twentieth century concept. Clearly, there were chemists doing things of that nature one hundred years ago, although I think that it could be argued that many of the important synthetic discoveries of the nineteenth century were serendipitous, but the primary role of a chemist in the nineteenth century was analysing and thereby determining the chemical nature of natural substances. One of the great influences at the beginning of the nineteenth century was the Industrial Revolution; the development of mines and mineral resources meant that a vital role existed for chemists in analysing unknown mineral samples. An industrialist wanted to know "What is this sample? Has anyone found it before? Is it worth digging out of the ground?" If the last answer was "Yes", everyone was happy.

So analytical chemists needed to develop tests that could characterise samples and, if possible, a 'unique' test that would test for only one substance. I wanted to demonstrate to you an example of a good nineteenth century analytical test and I thought it appropriate that one of the best unique tests is one which some of you may recall from the very first meeting of Holmes with Watson. When Dr. Watson is first introduced to Holmes in *A Study in Scarlet*, as a prospective flat sharer, Holmes ignores the normal pleasantries and drags Watson to his laboratory bench with the phrase "let us have some fresh blood". Holmes took a bodkin, of which I have a modern equivalent, and if I place it against my finger ......

CLICK!!!

...... I can generate a small quantity of blood.[1] Holmes continues "Now, I add this small quantity of blood to a litre of

---

[1] I had to do a similar experiment for a Christmas lecture series a few years back and found that adrenaline is very effective at preventing blood loss, so one has to actually work the finger to guarantee an adequate quantity of blood.

water. You perceive that the resulting mixture has the appearance of water. The proportion of blood cannot be more than one in a million". An accurate estimate if you consider that was a cubic millimetre in one thousand cubic centimetres. "I have no doubt, however, that we shall be able to obtain the characteristic reaction." And as he spoke he threw into the vessel some white crystals and then added a few drops of a transparent liquid. And the wonderful result of Sherlock Holmes' test was a mahogany red solution from which a brownish precipitate fell, and if we wait until the end of the lecture I can assure you that a small precipitate will fall. Holmes was modest enough to call it "the Sherlock Holmes test for haemoglobin". It was a 'unique' test for human haemoglobin, since it gives a reaction that no other substance does – no matter how old the haemoglobin, and no matter whether it is dried blood or not.[2] So there we have it, a perfect example of the nineteenth century analytical ideal, a test that is unique. Well, sadly most of the tests that the analytical chemist had were not quite as unique as that, but let us look at what they did have. They had water; how much of the substance dissolves in cold water, or hot? The test may not be a unique one, but the answer will be characteristic of any given substance.

What about acids? The acids feature quite liberally throughout Holmes' cases. There are unpleasant uses of sulphuric and prussic acids; there are the unpleasant

---

[2] I would also remind those of you that shortly afterwards Holmes observes that he deals in a lot of poisons and he really ought to put a plaster on his finger so I will copy his very sensible technique.

smells of hydrochloric acid. Holmes is left by Watson one evening, Holmes having claimed that a problem is soluble but he will need time. Watson disappears, has a busy day the following day, but returns eager to discover the solution to the problem. He walks in to their study and immediately enquires "Do you have the solution?" Holmes replies "Yes. It was bisulphate of baryta". He had spent all day working, not on the original problem, because he had solved that the previous evening, but instead studying a mineral sample seeking to establish its nature. I thought it would be nice if I could produce a small quantity of bisulphate of baryta for you this evening so I have prepared the following solutions. A clear colourless solution of barium hydroxide and a dilute solution of sulphuric acid. When I mix the two solutions together, immediately a white precipitate is produced. As far as inorganic chemistry is concerned, as insoluble a white material as you can produce. There is only one problem with this synthesis. It is my understanding that a bisulphate is formed by the precipitation of a Group I element, such as sodium, by sulphuric acid. Sadly baryta, i.e. barium, is a Group II element and as such has no bisulphate; it only has a sulphate. I fear that Conan Doyle perhaps had a slip of the pen in that particular case, but let us forgive him since it was a lovely example of a chemist deducing, by analysis, the nature of a mineral sample.

It remains true, however, that every substance had a characteristic reaction with each of the standard acids, nitric, hydrochloric and sulphuric. In addition, you could heat a sample or burn it in air. All of these tests will give some form of result, and by combination of all those tests an analytical chemist could derive the properties of any mineral sample. Then, by comparison with their own earlier results, or those of other chemists, they could determine whether the mineral was new, known or valuable.

But there were other, more subtle, tests developed by the nineteenth century chemists and I would like to show you one, beautiful example, for which I hope you will forgive me for indulging in what has been described as a filthy habit.[3]

Holmes was not only a practising scientist but also a published one. He wrote numerous monographs, on many subjects. He introduced the world to the characteristics of typewriters for example, but perhaps his most famous monograph was "upon the distinction between the ashes of various tobaccos". In this monograph he managed to develop tests to identify between one hundred and forty different forms of tobacco, a tremendous *tour de force.* I can reveal to you now that it is a little known fact that Holmes was invited to deliver a Friday evening discourse at the Royal Institution of Great Britain. I fear, in fact some of you may be aware, that there is a tradition of locking the lecturer within the lecturer's room before a discourse because of the fear that they will abscond. It was as a result of Holmes' discourse, where he did, in fact, feel obliged to depart with great haste because a case had come up which he felt merited

---

[3] At this point the lecturer lit a filter tipped cigarette and then stood it upon its filter to enable a length of ash to form.

immediate attention, that the Royal Institution of Great Britain was forced to adopt its rather Draconian attitude towards lecturers prior to the discourse. So Holmes never delivered his monograph on the distinction between various ashes but, after consulting with the librarian at the Royal Institution of Great Britain, I did discover that we have a copy of his famous monograph. For the last few weeks I have been working on some of the tests that he had developed and there are three really fundamental ones that I would like to show you. The first was to investigate the distinction between pipe tobacco, cigar tobacco and cigarette tobacco. So, if I take a small amount of pipe ash, a small amount of cigar ash and a small amount of cigarette ash I have now produced and place them into a separate one litre beaker, I can now make use of another wonderful colourless solution that Holmes had developed. If I add this solution to each of the three different ashes we find that pipe tobacco will produce a red solution, cigar tobacco a white solution and, in true patriotic style, cigarette tobacco will produce a blue solution.

But he went further and analysed within a single class of ashes. To illustrate this I have here a selection of six cigarette ashes. I obtained them from Bradley's in Oxford Street, which is just around the corner from the Royal Institution of Great Britain, and dissolved the ashes, each to produce a simple solution. Here I have a selection of Turkish, American, Russian, Armenian tobaccos prepared with different papers, different curing techniques, the addition of different chemicals. For each cigarette the manufacturing is consistent and unique.

What Holmes had perfected was a simple method of processing these solutions so that when ignited each burns with a characteristic, and uniquely different, colour.[4]

Holmes' monograph was truly remarkable, since he was able to determine the differences, not only between the various forms of tobacco but also between examples of each class. I spent many days working on his monograph, understanding the methods and reproducing his results, but as you know we at the Royal Institution of Great Britain have a reputation for bangs, sparks and flames, and I fear that in the course of my work the monograph was, sadly, destroyed. I hope that, if I have time and my memory serves me well enough, I will be able to recreate the wonderful science that it contained.

There is one final test from the monograph that I would like to share with you, because with it, I believe, Holmes extended his analytical tests into a different realm. Contained within a little known addendum to the paper was a test for examining the ashes of manuscripts. Holmes' startling conclusion was that not only can one analyse the paper and the ink but one could also determine the very quality of the writing that was involved. So I took the liberty of collecting some of the ashes from his own monograph and, utilising the 'Holmes test of quality penmanship', we can readily establish today that Holmes' monograph was a truly

---

[4] At this point the lecturer ignited six separate solutions, each of which burned with a different flame colour to which, sadly, no photographic reproduction can do justice.

illuminating piece of science.[5]

At this point I would ask you to remember my opening remarks relating to truth and embellishments but each of the tests that I have just shown you is a real technique, available to the analytical chemist of today.

These tests are generally used to test for a known substance, so how did the nineteenth century chemists isolate the new elements that were waiting to be discovered? The great revolution, to my mind, began at the end of the eighteenth century with the invention or discovery of the battery.

Prior to 1800, electricity had been known about for thousands of years, though we always give credit to the Greeks because they wrote about it. But, once more, I am sure it was known long before the Greeks that friction between glass-like substances, specifically amber, and a natural cloth or fur would generate an attractive force, i.e. attract small objects to it. It was Queen Elizabeth I's physician, William Gilbert, who wrote the first major monograph on electricity and magnetism. It was he who decided that an appropriate name for these effects would be electricity, from 'electron', the Greek word for amber. But it was not until the discoveries of Volta and Galvani in the latter part of the eighteenth century that electricity could be generated in quantities useful to chemistry. A battery will generate a far lower voltage than a simple

---

[5] Herewith the lecturer added a few ashes to yet another colourless solution, which immediately became suffused with a pale green phosphorescence.

frictional electricity machine, but it generates a far greater current, and current is the key to chemistry.

How, then, did the battery enter the world of the analytical chemist? Well, chemists haven't changed all that much over the years and even today if somebody presents a chemist with a new analytical technique, what do they do? They go to the shelf in the laboratory and take down every bottle there, stick it into the new machine and see if anything interesting happens!

What, then, were the first things they tried? Pure water is very little affected by electricity for the simple reason that in pure water there is nothing to carry the electricity, but this is dramatically altered once we add anything that is split, in solution, to form charged particles, called ions. Take, for example, a dilute solution of sulphuric acid and apply approximately ten volts, the sort of thing you get from a PP9 battery, and as you can see the solution begins to give off bubbles. At first sight you might assume that the solution is boiling, heated by the passage of electricity in the same way as a light bulb. But if I place my hands on the outside of the vessel I can show you that the water is still cold. To demonstrate the nature of the gas being produced, I have here a little soap solution cupped in the palm of my hand and I can collect some of the bubbles, the soap is simply to collect and retain the bubbles. Well, there are many tests that I could perform but I mentioned earlier that flammability was one of the simplest ......

BANG!!!

...... and that, for those of you who remember your days of chemical training, is often described as a 'pop' in chemistry text books, but if you have hydrogen mixed with oxygen in reasonable quantities the result is somewhat more than a 'pop'.

The introduction of the match proves that what we have done is to split water, not just heat it. We have split the water molecule, that is H_2O, into its constituent parts of hydrogen and oxygen. On applying the match, we have returned it to water by burning.

It was found, therefore, very early on that electricity from a battery could cause chemistry to occur. But the chemistry caused was of a very special nature, electricity tended to allow a chemist to reverse what is usually a spontaneous reaction. Water does not spontaneously split into its component parts at room temperature, but electricity can be used to drive that self-same reaction. Very rapidly chemists discovered that this was a general principal of electrolysis (literally the splitting by electricity). But this technique was not always as negative as the word 'splitting' suggests. All of the simple acids can be electrolysed, some splitting water to yield hydrogen and oxygen, others yielding a component of the acid such as chlorine from hydrochloric acid. But the principal applies to any ionic solution. I have here a concentrated solution of zinc bromide, a simple salt. If we pass an electric current through this solution, we do not see any gas being evolved, but instead a dark brown liquid dropping from one electrode and from the other beautiful, fern-like, growths of what we discover is pure metallic zinc. This electrolytic reaction is now not of academic interest but of true industrial importance; commercially available mineral ores can be transformed directly into metallic form without the need for smelting and chemical reduction. The development of aluminium as a commercial material in the nineteenth century was entirely dependent upon the electrolysis of aluminium ores and, to this day, the equivalent of nearly 10% of the National Grid's output is consumed in the electrolysis of salt water to generate chlorine gas for industrial use.

The application of electricity to solutions revolutionised the entire field of chemistry because, for the first time, there was a non-chemical process that could affect chemistry. This was the birth of electro-chemistry, and the person who, I feel, did most in this field, in the shortest period of time, was a previous director of the Royal Institution of Great Britain. In the years 1807−1808 seven elements were discovered in the world, six of them in this building by Sir Humphry Davy **(Figure 2)**. In passing I should note that Davy "was a malodorous chemist", a beautiful phrase coined by Conan Doyle to describe Holmes on occasions, and if you get a chance to explore the ambulatory here at the Royal Institution of Great Britain you will see a Gilray cartoon **(Figure 3)** of a lecture at the Royal Institution of Great Britain where Davy is seen assisting in the demonstration of the effects of 'laughing gas' (nitrous oxide), the discovery of which had made Davy's name when he worked at the Bristol Pneumatics Institute. The anaesthetic properties of nitrous oxide were discovered later but Davy and his friends did enjoy taking it for its mildly entertaining

Figure 2 – Sir Humphry Davy who became 'Professor of Chemistry' at the Royal Institution of Great Britain at the age of twenty-three. (Reproduced Courtesy of the Library, the Royal Institution of Great Britain)

Figure 3 – Cartoon by James Gilray, 1802. It shows Dr. Garnett experimenting upon Sir J. C. Hippesley with (Sir) Humphry Davy, who is holding the bellows, assisting. (*Famous Chemists: The Men and their Work*, Sir William A. Tilden, F.R.S., D.Sc., LL.D., Sc.D., George Routledge & Sons, Ltd., New York, 1921)

effects, but as you will observe in the cartoon, we are made well aware of one of the unpleasant side effects, and hence the 'malodorous' epithet. I will leave it to your curiosity to make the connection.

Davy discovered six elements by doing exactly what I have described; he went to the shelf in his laboratory and took down every bottle and he passed a current through it and he saw what happened. He passed a current through potash (potassium hydroxide) and produced metallic potassium; he passed it through soda (sodium hydroxide) and produced metallic sodium and he passed it through lime and other salts to generate calcium, magnesium, strontium and barium. In little over a year he had turned the second and third sections of Mrs. Marcet's list of 'elements' from what were compounds into pure metallic elements. Silicon, to this day, is primarily extracted by the electrolysis of sand.

Davy was joined at the Royal Institution of Great Britain, some years later, by a young book-binder's apprentice called Michael Faraday (**Figure 4**). Davy always said that his greatest discovery was Michael Faraday and I think that is almost undeniable. Davy was a great chemist but Faraday was something else. One of the first things that Davy and Faraday did was to embark on a grand tour of Europe and, despite the Napoleonic wars, they met the Great Emperor. Napoleon had aluminium tableware, noteworthy because of its extreme expense since it had to be chemically extracted. It was later on that electrolysis was used to extract aluminium in large quantities and today aluminium cutlery is no longer a sign

Figure 4 – Michael Faraday. (*Old and New London: A Narrative of its History, its People, and its Places,* Volume IV, Edward Walford, Cassell Peter & Galpin, London, Paris & New York, 1893)

of such extravagance.

One of the most significant things that Davy and Faraday did on their journey, while they were in Italy, was to prove that diamonds were made from carbon. If you think about it, there is no obvious reason for believing that diamonds and graphite, in the form of coal or charcoal, contain the same single chemical element. In my hand, I hold a half carat diamond kindly supplied to me by the De Beers company. You are all aware of what a diamond looks like; it certainly does not look like the lead of your pencil. How would you establish that diamond and graphite are composed of the same element? Well, we all know what happens if we heat graphite in air; it burns and generates carbon dioxide. Davy and Faraday took a diamond, placed it within a sealed vessel of oxygen, and using a large lens, focused the light of the sun to heat the diamond and burn it. They then measured the gaseous product and proved, for the first time, that it was in fact carbon dioxide.

What then would happen if we heated this diamond in air? Sadly not a great deal; the concentration of oxygen is so low in air that the burning is relatively slow and unimpressive, but if we take a source of concentrated oxygen, and here I have liquid oxygen, we have the opportunity to increase the rate of combustion dramatically. Well the sun is not out tonight, and it would take rather a long time anyway, so rather than that I am going to heat this diamond in a gas flame. As I mentioned, it is a half carat diamond, and were it perfectly cut I have been assured by my contact at De Beers that it would be worth something in the order of a thousand pounds, but never mind. If I heat it to incandescence, you can see that, when dropped into the goblet of pure liquid oxygen, the diamond burns. The diamond, although it is in a liquid at minus two hundred degrees Celsius, is heated to in excess of two thousand degrees by the burning process, it is liberating carbon dioxide, which is cooled within the liquid oxygen and at the end, if you come and look you will find the white carbon dioxide floating around within the liquid oxygen that remains.

Faraday was, as I mentioned, a truly remarkable scientist: a leading researcher in numerous fields, an advisor to governments and an influential figure in all aspects of nineteenth century British science. Although he joined the Royal Institution of Great Britain after Davy's work on electrolysis, he did in fact go on to lay the practical foundations of the entire subject of electrochemistry. It was he who demonstrated that, for a given chemical system, the amount of material converted by an electrical current was proportional to the total number of electrons that flow. By using this fact scientists were able to determine, for the first time, accurate relative masses for the various atomic elements. Faraday's work in this field is, even today, recognised on the reverse side of the current British £20 note (**Figure 5**). If you look very closely, I would almost recommend a magnifying glass, at the small print on the wall behind Faraday there is a series of words. These are the words that Faraday coined to describe the processes involved in electrochemistry; electrolysis, cation, anion and electrolyte.

If we look again at Mrs. Marcet's list, this time converting the layout to something more familiar, we can see the true elemental substances known about in 1803 (**Figure 6**), a total of 32 elements. But within sixty or seventy years the periodic list had expanded to double this size (**Figure 7**). Here we can see the elements that Davy discovered; sodium, potassium, magnesium, strontium, barium and calcium. Together they form the basis of the first two groups on the table, groups which were previously unknown. The other members of the first two groups of elements were discovered, not by Davy, but by other chemists using very similar techniques.

There was a great expansion in the number of metallic elements situated in the centre of the table and chemists continued in their process of observation, measurement and deduction.

Figure 5 (Overleaf) – The current £20 note which features a portrait of Michael Faraday (from a drawing by Roger Withington), as well as him lecturing at one of the Royal Institution of Great Britain Christmas Lectures, complete with magneto-electric spark apparatus in the foreground. The obverse has patterns based on bar magnets and iron filings, and a purple square, to assist the visually handicapped, in the form of the benzene molecule. The Royal Institution of Great Britain is represented by a sun pattern taken from the coat of arms and a representation of the decorative plaster border of the central dome in the main lecture theatre. (Reproduced Courtesy of the Issue Office, Bank of England, London)

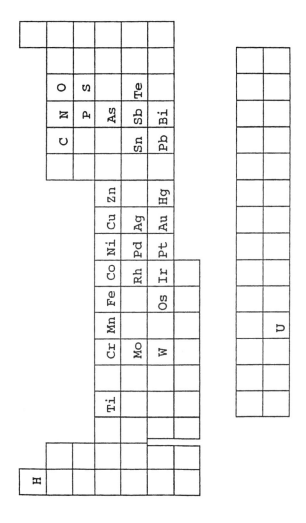

Figure 6 — The Periodic Table *circa* 1800.

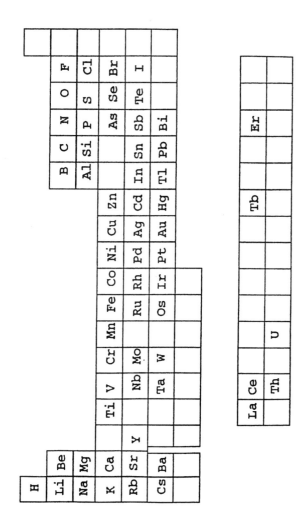

Figure 7 — The Periodic Table *circa* 1860.

One of the things that soon became apparent was that there were patterns or, as they were known, periods, in the properties of the elements and their compounds.

If you study the elements you find that whilst lithium, sodium, potassium, rubidium and caesium are different, they are certainly very similar in many respects. Particularly, they come in similar combinations, that is they combine with other elements in the same proportions. Two atoms of each of these elements combine with one of oxygen. When we look at beryllium, magnesium, calcium, strontium and barium, only one atom of each element combines with a single atom of oxygen.

Let us consider the group of six metallic elements near the centre of the table, ruthenium, rhodium, palladium, iridium, osmium and platinum. These were known as the noble metals and they were found, almost invariably, together in the same mineral sources. They have very similar properties, both physical and chemical. One of the most intriguing is in fact not so much their chemical reactivity, but that they all have the remarkable property that they could modify, and in some cases accelerate, chemical reactions between other elements. They are not in themselves consumed by chemical reactions but they can alter the rate of reaction. I have here a small bottle containing charcoal covered with just 5% platinum, a very small proportion of platinum. If I take some of the charcoal and add it to one of my conventional bottles ......

BANG!!!

...... we can initiate what is undoubtedly the most horrendous experiment this evening! I assure you that the platinum is not consumed in the process, and were we able to track down those bits we would find that all the platinum was intact. It simply accelerates the reaction and any of the elements from that region would perform a similar function if added to the obligatory mixture of hydrogen and oxygen.

If we look at the halogens i.e., fluorine, chlorine, bromine and iodine, they are most notable for how they differ from most other elements in appearance. Almost all the elements in the table are shiny silvery metals, with only copper and gold being coloured. The halogens on the right-hand side are clearly different; chlorine is a distinctly green gas, bromine, which we observed liberated in solution earlier, is a brown gas and iodine, if I heat it a little, has a distinct purplish tinge. Chemists quickly realised that there were many groups of elements that had either similar properties, such as fixed combinations, or systematically varying properties such as reactivity. A vital insight into these results was made when people began writing out the list of known elements in ascending order of atomic weight. Now the elements that seemed to be associated seemed to occur at regular intervals, or periods, down the list. How did chemistry rationalise these seemingly disparate pieces of evidence that seemed to point to some underlying pattern?

Now, I thought at this point I would perhaps highlight the idea of observation, measurement and deduction with a suitable quote, but there are so many and it would seem arbitrary to pick one over the other, but purely by chance, several days ago, I was flicking through the current edition of *Science* and my eye was struck by a cartoon **(Figure 8)**. Maybe this summarises my understanding of the 'scientific' method. This cartoon appealed to me particularly because the more observant among you may have noticed that I have tobacco stains on my fingers. In addition paint on my trousers and plaster on my shoes is, sadly, all too common. I would, however, like to give Holmes one quotation, from *The Blanched Soldier* to summarise his 'scientific' method:

> "'The process,' said I, 'starts upon the supposition that when you have eliminated all which is impossible, then whatever remains, however improbable, must be the truth. It may well be that several explanations remain, in which case one tries test after test until one or other of them has a convincing amount of support'".

Whilst this is perhaps one of the most famous, and most misquoted, phrases from Sherlock Holmes which describes his methods, I think that you would agree that it is an excellent definition of the 'scientific' method in general. Chemists spent much of the nineteenth century observing and measuring the properties of materials derived from nature. From those results they could deduce the elements contained within a given sample, but

Figure 8 – A 'Doylean' cartoon which illustrates the 'scientific method'. (Reproduced Courtesy of *Science,* September - October, 1994)

in addition, occasionally, they were faced with a remarkable situation. From the results they could deduce the presence of an element that their observations and measurements could not identify and they were forced to a single conclusion, namely that they had discovered a new element. It was therefore by Holmes' method and Holmes' process of logical deduction that the list of elements expanded inexorably.

As I have already stated, a vital insight into these results was made when people began tabulating the list of known elements in ascending order of atomic mass (as determined by Faraday's electrochemical technique), and found that the elements that seemed to be associated by their properties seemed to occur at regular intervals, or periods, within the list. The question still remained of how could chemistry rationalise these seemingly disparate pieces of evidence?

Many chemists tried, many chemists studied the various properties of the elements that were known and many came up with suggestions for how these patterns could be used, but the chemist that got it right and had the courage of his convictions to use his theory as a predictive tool is perhaps my hero in this detective story.

His portrait is behind me and some of you might recognise Dmitri Ivanovich Mendeleyev (**Figures 9 & 10**). Ever since I first worked at the Royal Institution of Great Britain, I have loved his portrait and in preparing this talk I hoped that I would be able to find a description of Moriarty which fitted this remarkable image. Sadly the

Figure 9 – Dmitri Mendeleyev (1834-1907), a Russian chemist, who discovered the 'Periodic Law'. (*Great Chemists*, Edited by Eduard Farber, Interscience Publishers, New York and London, 1961)

Figure 10 — Statue of Dmitri Mendeleyev standing outside the entrance to Moscow State University. (Antony
Richards, 1998)

one detailed description of Moriarty that I could find starts with the observation that he was clean shaven, and therefore I must settle for the suggestion that this is how Holmes looked in one of his legendary disguises, or maybe how Moriarty felt after loosing out to Holmes in one of their intellectual battles. It is a wonderful picture and I am proud to say that I persuaded Professor Thomas, a previous director of the Royal Institution of Great Britain, to allow me to hang a portrait Mendeleyev in my office where it now looks down upon my every working day.

What Mendeleyev did was to use the observed periodic properties to tabulate the known elements in, approximately, ascending order of atomic mass. He was not the first chemist to do so and he found, as others had found before him, that the system did not work perfectly. The two most notable problems were, firstly, that in order for the periods to be absolutely adhered to, the rule of ascending atomic mass had to be occasionally broken (hence the word 'approximately' in my earlier sentence) and, secondly, that gaps appeared in the table where no known elements existed. As many of you will have already observed, the tables of the elements that I have been using in this lecture have been based upon his ideas, and I once again draw your attention to those elements known in the 1860's (**Figure 7**).

Mendeleyev was not the first to make this attempt, but all previous chemists had taken these problems to be fatal to the idea that periodic properties indicated an underlying pattern. Mendeleyev had the courage of his convictions to conclude that the known chemistry must be wrong in two respects. First, there must be some error in the determined atomic masses due to some unknown property of elements, and second that the gaps in the table were indicating the existence of yet more elements that were waiting to be discovered. It was now that Mendeleyev took his process of deduction to its logical conclusion; by virtue of the periodic properties that underlie the table, he was able to predict the properties of the three elements required to fill the first three gaps. He was able to predict many of the major properties of these elements and these predictions helped guide chemists in their subsequent search.

Happily, luck was with Mendeleyev and, within the next ten years, all three were discovered. Scandium, gallium and germanium. His predictions were so accurate, and the predictive power of his periodic table was so great, that he was universally acclaimed for his discovery. It has to be said that he was somewhat fortunate in certain respects. I will not go into precise details but he was fortunate that he chose to make a number of predictions and the ones he chose were the ones that turned out to be correct. Thankfully he had no knowledge of the noble, or inert, gases which were in fact largely discovered here at the Royal Institution of Great Britain by Sir James Dewar at the turn of the century as their masses would have increased the approximate nature of the required ordering. Mendeleyev lectured here at the Royal Institution of Great Britain in 1889 on 'An Attempt to Apply to Chemistry One of the Principles of Newton's Natural Philosophy'. It is reproduced in the *Proceedings of the Royal Institution,* volume XII, page 506, for those of you who wish to discover to which of Newton's principles he is referring.

I came upon the fact that another Holmes gave a lecture at the Royal Institution of Great Britain in 1899 **(Figure 11)**. This was Sir Richard Rivington Holmes who gave a discourse entitled 'George the Third as a Collector'. It is a little known fact that Sherlock and Mycroft had an older brother (I can find no reference to him in Dr. Watson's accounts) who was the curator of the King's library at Windsor. He was 12 years older than Mycroft so Holmes' father was clearly quite elderly by the time Sherlock came along. By all accounts Sir Richard's knowledge of antiquities, the arts and royal collections was world famous and renowned. He gave a most erudite discourse and it contained some lovely comments about George III himself. If you remember your history, or have perhaps seen the recent play and film of his life, you will appreciate the comment contained within the opening paragraph of the lecture:

> "The stormy political quarrels at home and the complication of events abroad have combined to cast into oblivion the early cultivated tastes and pursuits of the King, as in later years the dark clouds of disease obscured the finer workings of his brain."

Perhaps these days it would not be phrased so kindly.

WEEKLY EVENING MEETING,

Friday, February 17, 1899.

Sir Frederick Bramwell, Bart., D.C.L. LL.D. F.R.S., Honorary
Secretary and Vice-President, in the Chair.

Richard R. Holmes, Esq., M.V.O. F.S.A.

George the Third as a Collector.

The subject of this discourse I have chosen particularly because
it is one which has in most histories either been passed over entirely,
or treated with indifference. It is generally disposed of in a few curt
phrases taken from the pages of contemporary diarists, repeated by
every subsequent writer as containing everything necessary to be
recorded of the King's tastes and epitomising his character with
epigrammatic smartness, but seldom verified by examination or research.
The stormy political quarrels at home and the complication of events
abroad have combined to cast into oblivion the early cultivated tastes
and pursuits of the King, as in later years the dark clouds of disease
obscured the finer workings of his brain.

To appreciate fully the extent and value of the collections by
which George III. has permanently enriched the possessions of the
Crown, it is as well to consider briefly the condition in which His
Majesty found the ancestral treasure of his Royal house when he
succeeded his grandfather on the throne. Spoliation and robbery
had played sad havoc among them, and it is only wonderful that
anything of value was left at all. The nation perhaps may be con-
gratulated that, on the foundation of the British Museum, the ancient
library of the Kings of England was transferred there by George II.,
and so escaped the fate of many of the treasures of the Crown. In a
note prefixed to a MS. catalogue of the pictures of Queen Anne by
Horace Walpole, who once owned the volume, he says :—

" As several pictures mentioned in the following catalogue have
not appeared in any of the palaces within my memory I imagine
many were taken away by different persons between the death of
Queen Anne and the arrival of George I. Henrietta Lady Suffolk
told me that Queen Caroline never had any of Queen Anne's jewels
but one pearl necklace. George I., who hated her and his son, might
give what he found to the Duchess of Kendal. Her niece, Lady
Chesterfield, certainly had several large diamonds. Catherine of
Braganza, widow of Charles II., carried away several of the pictures
of the Crown of Portugal. A Lord Chamberlain pawned the Vandyke
hangings at Houghton to a banker, who, many years after, they not

Vol. XVI. (No. 93.)   F

Figure 11 — Extract of the discourse text as given by
Richard R. Holmes, M.V.O., F.S.A. at the Royal Institution
of Great Britain in 1899. (*The Proceedings of the
Royal Institution of Great Britain,* Volume XVI, Royal
Institution of Great Britain, London, 1899)

So where did Mendeleyev's discovery take science? Well, science continued apace. I mentioned that there remained a number of difficulties with the periodic table. Those were resolved as later researchers studied the building blocks of the elements themselves, but that is really within the realm of nuclear physics. In chemistry, the periodic table became the foundation of all research. Chemists were able to use the periodic table as a guide and have managed to fill in every single gap that remained in Mendeleyev's table. The properties of elements could be rationalised and used to predict their behaviour in previously unimagined circumstances, for example many of you will have a catalytic converter in the exhaust system of your car. It is essentially a ceramic honeycomb covered with a black powder similar to that which I used to initiate my last detonation. The precise mixture is a closely guarded secret of the Johnson-Matthey company, but it was developed from a knowledge of the catalytic properties of those metals at the base of the periodic table.

Chemists are sometimes frustrated by the fact that the periodic table offers a limited set of elements with a finite set of properties. Physicists rarely accept the confines of nature and one of the great revolutions of the late twentieth century has been founded upon the discovery that in the world of physics the periodic table can be used to tailor the electronic properties of solids to our needs. The semiconductor industry is based upon the use of silicon, derived by electrolysis from sand, and I have here a block of 99.9999% pure silicon. Silicon is a natural semiconductor, as is the element below it in the periodic table, germanium, and, in fact, the one above it, carbon, although carbon's bandgap is so large that at room temperature it is regarded as an electronic insulator. But the silicon used in electronic components has its properties modified by the inclusion of trace amounts of other elements, most commonly the elements on either side of it in the periodic table, aluminium and phosphorus to produce p-type and n-type semiconductors respectively. But the story does not end here. The elements above and below aluminium and phosphorus have similar properties and can also be used.

Many of you will have a compact disc player and within that you will find a semiconductor laser that has been fabricated from alternate layers of gallium arsenide and gallium aluminium arsenide, semiconductors similar to silicon but with the remarkable property of being able to emit light. You will all see immediately that the number of combinations of elements from this region of the periodic table is enormous, and I can assure you that physicists all over the world are trying all of the possible mixtures to create the semiconductors required in the rapidly advancing field of electronics. Because of the way in which the electronic properties of large collections of atoms combine, physicists are, in effect, creating new electronic elements with properties in between those of the pure elements.

Even in the world of pure chemistry the periodic table is not finished. Our understanding of nuclear reactions is such that we can now synthesise truly new elements. The comprehensive periodic table **(Figure 12)** indicates those elements that do not occur naturally on Earth but have

H																	He
Li	Be											B	C	N	O	F	Ne
Na	Mg											Al	Si	P	S	Cl	Ar
K	Ca	Sc	Ti	V	Cr	Mn	Fe	Co	Ni	Cu	Zn	Ga	Ge	As	Se	Br	Kr
Rb	Sr	Y	Zr	Nb	Mo	Tc	Ru	Rh	Pd	Ag	Cd	In	Sn	Sb	Te	I	Xe
Cs	Ba	Lu	Hf	Ta	W	Re	Os	Ir	Pt	Au	Hg	Tl	Pb	Bi	Po	At	Rn
Fr	Ra	Lr															

La	Ce	Pr	Nd	Pm	Sm	Eu	Gd	Tb	Dy	Ho	Er	Tm	Yb
Ac	Th	Pa	U	Np	Pu	Am	Cm	Bk	Cf	Es	Fm	Md	No

Figure 12 — The Periodic Table *circa* 1990.

had to be synthesised *via* nuclear reactions. Many of them are derived from the decay of heavier elements, but we can build up new, heavier elements, at great cost in terms of time and money. Why do we do it? Well, partly because we can, partly because it expands our knowledge of the periodic properties of all the elements, and partly because there are reasons to believe that there may exist even heavier elements that will be truly stable and therefore be available for chemists to use in conventional chemistry. A truly tempting opportunity that hasn't been available to chemistry for well over 50 years.

What would Holmes be doing today? What techniques would he be using? Well I am sure he would use all of the modern techniques of analytical chemistry. Perhaps no longer the simple Holmes test for haemoglobin, but the modern equivalents like the electron microscope, the mass spectrograph and D.N.A. profiling. Holmes, I am sure, would be proud to be able to add these to his techniques, and to his remarkable intellect in his pursuit of the truth.

On the other hand I would like to stress what has, perhaps, been the theme running through the whole of this lecture. Holmes was clearly a chemist, not just an able chemist, he was a chemist with a profound knowledge of chemistry, as Watson observed. But I think he was more than that. He was not just a chemist, he was the epitome of a chemist. He used analytical techniques to analyse, observe and deduce the nature of a sample, a situation, a case. Sir Arthur Conan Doyle used the model of the nineteenth century chemist using analytical techniques and transposed it to the world of crime. Applying what was at the time perhaps the purest of scientific disciplines, the purest of techniques, to a world perhaps of more interest to the ordinary everyday reader.

Holmes was not just an analytical chemist, he was *The Analytical Chemist.* He was truly a man of his time.

Bibliography

The Complete Sherlock Holmes, Sir Arthur Conan Doyle, Blitz Editions (undated).

Conversations on Chemistry; in which the elements of that science are familiarly explained and illustrated by experiments, Mrs. Marcet, Longman, Orme, Brown, Green, & Longman, London (1803).

Faraday And Holmes: Two Chemists, One Character

Doctor Antony J. Richards, M.R.I.

It is not unusual for people, when young, to have idols or heroes. Depending on the era these tend to be singers or pop stars, sporting personalities, often footballers, stage and screen actors and actresses, and more recently those from the world of television. I am no different in this respect, though two of my heroes, unlike many others, have not faded in popularity as I have aged. My first icon is one of the foremost scientists the world has ever known, and perhaps the greatest singular experimentalist of all time, while the second is a fictional character created by the pen of Sir Arthur Conan Doyle and justifiably the best known and most imitated detective of all time. I refer, of course, to Michael Faraday and Sherlock Holmes.

It was not until I came to have a hand in the writing of 'Holmes, Chemistry and the Royal Institution' that I realised that these two personalities were not only of similar character, but also led, in many ways, parallel lives. Below I have listed, in no particular order, a 'Baker Street' dozen areas which illustrate my assertion and which, I hope, will be of interest to the reader.

(1) Men Of Science

Faraday and Holmes were undoubtedly scientists of the first order. Beyond this they were both chemists and surpassing this further, they were both experimental chemists. The comparison does not stop there, for both men were only interested in science for the sake of science itself, which is something of a paradox since most of their research converged towards practical applications.

In the case of Faraday, there was the work on the invention of a lamp which could be used safely in mines. He had a large hand in the testing of what later became known as the 'Davy Lamp'. In the 1820's, Faraday analysed a large number of gunpowders for the 'East India Company' and was called upon to give expert testimony at many trials. He was also involved in the not so successful attempt to stop the corrosion of the copper sheeting on British warships. The solution of adding zinc to the copper cladding retarded the corrosion, but unfortunately created a new problem in that, whereas copper salts are poisonous to marine life, the addition of zinc caused barnacles and the like to adhere to the bottom of ships with the resulting loss in steerage.

Hence it can be seen that Faraday was one of the first people to bring science and technology together. The above examples interested Faraday, but one that did not was the long period of consultancy work for the 'Board of Longitude', which was funded through the Government. The aim of the work, originally set up by Davy, was to improve the quality of optical glass which would aid navigation at sea. Faraday made two hundred and fifteen different pieces of glass, which were cut by George Dolland the optician, and tested by John Herschel the astronomer. This, and his other various appointments in the early 1830's, brought in an income in the region of five hundred pounds, while his work in the law courts as an expert witness was estimated to be worth a further thousand pounds a year. However, after Davy died, in 1829, Faraday lost no time in freeing himself, the following year, of this tiresome work so that he could move on to things that were of more interest to him, even though it meant a reduction in his income.

As a further example of work that interested Faraday for the sake of the work itself consider his greatest achievement, electromagnetic induction, which he actually discovered only two months after stopping his work on glasses. There was no practical aim to this work at its commencement, other than to investigate this phenomenon. It led to the electric motor and was responsible for moulding the way our modern world functions. Certainly Faraday, on making the discovery, had little idea of its full importance. It has been variously reported that, when trying to explain the value of this new discovery to Chancellor of the Exchequer W. E. Gladstone (or it may have been to Prime Minister Robert Peel), he was asked the practical use of it. The reputed answer by Faraday was that "Why sir, there is a probability that you will soon be able to tax it".

Faraday could undoubtedly have become a rich man from his scientific achievements, but it was the work itself that was its own reward. There are numerous examples to show that Holmes also lived and worked solely for the sake of his art, which included his chemistry. When the reader is first introduced to Holmes in *A Study in Scarlet* he is working on some chemical experiment at St. Bartholomew's Hospital, which transpires to be a replacement for the old guaiacum test for blood detection. In this case, as with others, some pure research by Holmes had a very practical application. As Holmes modestly puts it: "Had this test been invented, there are hundreds of men now walking the earth who would long ago have paid the penalty of their crimes. ... Now we have the Sherlock Holmes test, and there will no longer be any difficulty".

Young Stamford, in describing Sherlock Holmes to Dr. Watson at the Holborn Restaurant, said that he was "an enthusiast in some branches of science" and "a first-rate chemist".

Chemistry was certainly a passion for him; in *The Gloria Scott*, while Holmes is at college, he returned from Donnithorpe to his London rooms during the long summer vacation where he "spent seven weeks working out a few experiments in organic chemistry".

Another scientific connection between the two men is Montpellier[1]. Holmes "spent some months in a research into the coal-tar derivatives, which I conducted in a laboratory at Montpelier, in the south of France", according to Dr. Watson in *The Empty House*. Faraday also visited the town while on his scientific 'Grand Tour' of Europe with Davy. Faraday recorded in his diary that he was even allowed to walk around the fort despite France being at war with Great Britain at that time.

---

[1] Montpelier was the spelling used by Conan Doyle.

(2) London

Both Faraday and Holmes are inextricably linked with London. Both were resident, for the most celebrated periods of their life, within the City of Westminster: Faraday in Albemarle Street and Holmes in Baker Street. In fact, until Faraday was invited by Davy to accompany him on his scientific tour of Europe, he had travelled no further than twelve miles from London.

Faraday was born at Newington Butts, which was then in Surrey, but as a child moved to Jacob's Well Mews, Manchester Square, where the Wallace Collection is now housed. Incidentally, the collection includes paintings by Emile Jean Horace Vernet, who, it will be recalled, was related to Holmes since the detective's grandmother was Vernet's sister (as revealed in *The Greek Interpreter*).

Faraday worked as an errand boy for George Riebau, a bookseller and bookbinder, who had his premises in Blandford Street **(Figure 1)**. It will be recalled that Holmes led Watson down Blandford Street on their way to Camden House in *The Empty House*.

While at the Royal Institution of Great Britain, Faraday only left London twice for extended periods. The first was while undertaking the aforementioned 'Grand Tour' of Europe with Davy. The second was due to his declining health when he was advised to rest and he again went to

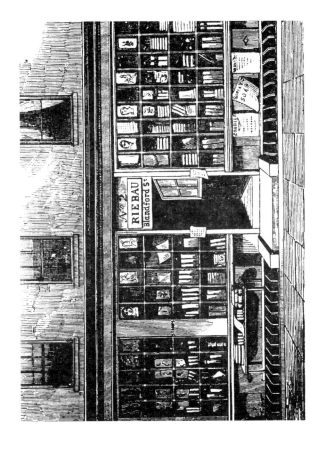

Figure 1 — Ribau's shop in Blandford Street. (*Michael Faraday: His Life and Work*, Silvanus P. Thompson, D.Sc., F.R.S., Cassell and Company, Ltd., London, Paris, New York & Melbourne, 1898)

Europe for several months. Other than this he only ventured away from the metropolis when on scientific business, such as his researches into better lighting for lighthouses, which took him to Dover and the South Coast, and his investigations into the Hasewell Colliery disaster near Durham.

Holmes travelled more extensively than Faraday throughout Europe and Southern England on his investigations, though it is clear from his comment in *The Priory School* that he did not necessarily relish such activities. Having been given a large cheque for services rendered to the Duke of Holderness, he sees a set of shoes for horses, shaped with a cloven foot of iron, so as to throw pursuers off the track, where upon Holmes remarks "It is the second most interesting object that I have seen in the North". Clearly Holmes, like Faraday, preferred the environs of London.

(3) Travel

In 1808 Davy received the Napoleon prize of three thousand francs for his work on electricity. Five years later, despite Great Britain still being at war with France, Davy was granted special dispensation by Napoleon to undertake an extended scientific tour of Europe. Faraday was invited to accompany the party as his secretary and scientific assistant. The party sailed from Plymouth and visited France, Italy, Switzerland, Germany and Belgium.

Among the cities visited by Faraday on the 'Grand Tour' were Lyons, Montpellier, Turin (which involved crossing the Alps), Florence and Geneva. Each of these cities was also visited by Holmes. In *The Reigate Squire*, Holmes sent a telegram from Lyons to Watson informing him that he was lying ill at the Hotel Dulong. It was in Montpellier, as already mentioned, that Holmes performed some chemical experiments into coal-tar derivatives, while Geneva[2] and the Alps were visited by both Holmes and Watson as they made their way to Reichenbach, pursued by Moriarty, in *The Final Problem*. Holmes went to Florence after his fateful meeting with Moriarty at the Reichenbach Falls during the 'Great Hiatus'.

It is interesting to note that in 1835, when exhausted from his work, Faraday left the Institution for eight months and chose Switzerland as a suitable place for recuperation.

(4) Lifestyle

The beauty of nature appealed to Faraday, especially landscapes which would move him to lyrical ecstasy. Although Watson writes in *The Cardboard Box* that "Appreciation of nature found no place among his many gifts", by the time of *The Lion's Mane* Holmes claims that in retirement he will give himself up entirely "to that soothing life of Nature for which I had so often yearned during the long years spent amid the gloom of London". Certainly this represented a change of attitude.

---

[2] It is interesting to note that Sir Humphrey Davy not only visited Geneva, but also died there and is buried at *le Cimetiere dr Plainpalais*.

Music was also important to both men. Faraday often visited the theatre or attended musical soirées. Watson described Holmes in *The Red-Headed League* as "an enthusiastic musician, being himself not only a very capable performer but a composer of no ordinary merit". He owned a Stradivarius and enjoyed opera (attending Wagner at Covent Garden in *The Red Circle*), concert music (as mentioned in *The Retired Colourman*, *The Hound of the Baskervilles* and *The Red-Headed League* to give but three examples), and even researched the obscure compositions of Orlandus Lassus (as revealed in *The Bruce-Partington Plans*).

Faraday was extremely astute at understanding dialects and languages. On one occasion, in the Vale of Neath, he engaged himself in conversation with a small girl. He was able to understand her, even though she spoke in a Welsh tongue. Holmes could not only disguise himself well but took on the entire character of a person, including any languages or dialects needed. He was able to speak as an Italian priest in *The Final Problem*, a French *ouvrier* in *The Disappearance of Lady Frances Carfax* and an Irish-American spy in *His Last Bow*.

Faraday tended to keep long hours; nine in the morning until eleven at night was not untypical. During this time he would not allow himself to be disturbed, and would only be helped by his assistant, Sergeant Charles Anderson. The laboratory was a silent place. Charles Wheatstone, in a letter to W. F. Cooke, dated 4th. October, 1838, gives an indication as to just how devoted to his work this man was:

"I called on Faraday this morning and was told that this was one of the days on which he denies himself to every body for the purpose of pursuing uninterruptedly his own researches. He - will be visible tomorrow".

Similarly, Holmes was in the habit of keeping long hours when on a case. He was not as a rule an early riser, as revealed in *The Speckled Band*, but there were also "those not infrequent occasions when he was up all night" at work, as in *The Hound of the Baskervilles*. Again, this comes across in *A Study in Scarlet* when Stamford tells Watson that Holmes "is sure to be at the laboratory" where "He either avoids the place for weeks, or else works there from morning till night". In the same narrative Holmes says that "I get in the dumps at times, and don't open my mouth for days on end" indicating that on occasion, like Faraday, he needed to work and think without interruption.

Neither men took exercise for its own sake. Holmes, though, was a fit person, being a good runner and possessing great strength as demonstrated when Holmes straightened the poker bent by Dr. Grimesby Roylott in *The Speckled Band*. The best description is, perhaps, given in *The Yellow Face*:

"Sherlock Holmes was a man who seldom took exercise for exercise's sake. Few men were capable of greater muscular effort, and he was undoubtedly one of the finest boxers of his weight that I have ever seen; but he looked upon aimless bodily exertion as a waste of energy, and he seldom bestirred himself save where there was some professional object to be served. Then he was absolutely untiring and indefatigable".

Faraday was also a fit man. He would, on occasion, cycle on his velocipede as far as Hampstead, and was known to take to the Thames in a rowing boat for picnics with his nieces. Even at the age of seventy, there is a report of him crossing fields and hedges, in snow and storm, in order to fulfil his duties for 'Trinity House' and visit various lighthouses on the South Coast.

Faraday had a period of exhaustion during the first half of the 1840's. On 7th. December, 1840 the Managers of the Royal Institution of Great Britain resolved that Faraday should consider himself "totally exonerated from all duties connected with the Royal Institution till his health should be completely re-established". This is when Faraday made his second, and final, visit outside the United Kingdom to Switzerland. Holmes also had health problems as revealed in *The Devil's Foot*:

"It was, then in the spring of the year 1897 that Holmes's iron constitution showed some symptoms of giving way in the face of constant hard work of a most exacting kind, aggravated, perhaps, by occasional indiscretions of his own".

It was Dr. Moore Agar, of Harley Street, who ordered Holmes to "surrender himself to complete rest if he wished to avert an absolute breakdown". Instead of Switzerland, Holmes travelled to a small cottage near Poldhu Bay where he was to become involved in the "Cornish horror".

(5) Education

Faraday received only an elementary education. His love of science was inspired by reading the 'Encyclopaedia Britannica' and Jane Marcet's book entitled 'Conversations in Chemistry' as well as attending meetings at the City Philosophical Society in Fleet Street.

It has been mentioned that the remainder of his scientific education was gained when Davy embarked on a scientific tour of Europe with Faraday as his assistant. Apart from this, Faraday was largely self-taught having received only a basic education:

> "My education was of the most ordinary description, consisting of little more than the rudiments of reading, writing, and arithmetic at a common day school. My hours out of school were passed at home and in the streets".

Holmes preferred to keep the *American Encyclopaedia* as mentioned in *The Five Orange Pips*. The small matter of Holmes' early education is very much open to debate. However, he did understand the value of a good education when he spoke to Watson enthusiastically about the Board schools in *The Naval Treaty*.

"'Look at those big, isolated clumps of buildings rising up above the slates, like islands in a lead-coloured sea.'

'The Board schools.'

'Lighthouses, my boy! Beacons of the future! Capsules, with hundreds of bright little seeds in each, out of which will spring the wiser, better England of the future'".

Faraday understood the value of education too and in 1862 gave evidence to the 'Public Schools Commission'. This was a 'Royal Commission' set up, with the Earl of Clarendon as chairman, to investigate the education given in Public schools. Faraday drew attention to the complete lack of science teaching and added that those who had received a traditional Public school education based on the classics were ignorant of natural science and, what made it worse, they did not realise that they were ignorant. He would no doubt have approved of the Board schools.

(6) High Society

Though his work was known to the majority of the general public of the Victorian era, Faraday was essentially a very private man uninterested in social ambition. He was given many honorary degrees from universities around the world. These he would always acknowledge after his name in the books he wrote, but apart from that he shunned publicity. It is telling that he insisted that his gravestone, at Highgate cemetery, should read simply

'Michael Faraday', along with the dates of his birth and death.

In many ways he was a recluse within the Royal Institution of Great Britain such was the importance of his work. However, on occasion, he would attend soirées at the salon of the wealthy philanthropist Baroness Burdett Coutts. He could also be found in Great Marlborough Street where he mingled with artists and musicians, among them J. W. M. Turner.

Holmes seems an altogether more complex character in this respect. He often left the credit for solving a case to the police, and then would complain at the lack of recognition he received. He also did not seek popular adoration as was made clear in _The Six Napoleons_: "The same singularly proud and reserved nature which turned away with disdain from popular notoriety was capable of being moved to its depths by spontaneous wonder and praise from a friend". Holmes had few friends, apart from Watson, and did not mix with high society, preferring, like Faraday, to remain at his work. Even between cases he would not mix with people, but turned instead to his seven-per-cent solution of cocaine. This almost reclusive nature started while at college (as revealed in _The Gloria Scott_):

> "'You never heard me talk of Victor Trevor?' he
> asked. 'He was the only friend I made during the
> two years I was at college. I was never a very
> sociable fellow, Watson, always rather fond of
> moping in my rooms and working out my own

little methods of thought, so that I never mixed much with the men of my year'".

(7) Honours

Although Faraday would accept honorary degrees he had little compunction about declining other high honours, in turning down invitations to socialise, or in avoiding interruptions. This included refusing the delegation that implored him to become 'President of the Royal Society'. He later noted in a letter:

> "Tyndall, I must remain plain Michael Faraday to the last; and let me now tell you, that if I accept the honour which the Royal Society desires to confer upon me, I would not answer for the integrity of my intellect for a single year".

He also refused the 'Presidency of the Chemical Society', and hardly ever attended their meetings though he lived but yards away. Although he declined the 'Professorship of Chemistry' in the new University of London in 1827, he agreed to serve as a member of the 'Senate' in which he took great pride.

Holmes, it will be recalled, also refused honours, including a knighthood in June 1902 as revealed by Watson in _The Three Garridebs_. However, in _The Golden Pince-Nez_, Holmes did accept the 'Legion of Honour' for the arrest of Huret, the Boulevard Assassin. An honour of a different kind was afforded to Holmes at the conclusion of _The Bruce-Partington Plans_:

"Some weeks afterwards I learned incidentally that
my friend spent a day at Windsor, whence he
returned with a remarkably fine emerald tie-pin.
When I asked him if he had bought it, he
answered that it was a present from a certain
gracious lady in whose interests he had once been
fortunate enough to carry out a small
commission".

Faraday was also one of the few English people ever to be
the recipient of the 'Legion of Honour'. As a strict
Sandemanian, and 'Elder' of his church, he was taught to
be humble and not to seek such rewards. However, he
once found himself subject to the strict discipline of his
Church: he was deprived of his Eldership and excluded
from being a member for a time. The reason for this
action was that Faraday had been absent one Sunday
without a good enough reason, and had not been
sufficiently penitent when rebuked. It later transpired that
he had been invited to dine with Queen Victoria at
Windsor that day, though it is not known whether he
received any mark of favour on that occasion.

(8) Common Place Book

Faraday was guided by the advice given on self-
improvement in *The Improvement of the Mind* by Isaac
Watts and kept a 'common place book' in which he
jotted down ideas, facts, quotations and questions as they
occurred to him. The inscription in the earliest book
reads:

"A Collection of Notices, Occurrences, Events etc., relating to the Arts and Sciences collected from the Public Papers, Reviews, Magazines and other miscellaneous works. Intended to promote both Amusement and Instruction and also corroborate or invalidate those theories which are continually starting in the world of science".

Holmes, it will be recalled, also kept several 'common place books' which he frequently used. One volume was devoted to biographies and another was filled with the agony columns from the various London papers. For instance, it is recorded that Holmes looked up the biography of Irene Adler in *The Scandal in Bohemia* and found it "sandwiched in between that of a Hebrew Rabbi and that of a staff-commander who had written a monograph upon the deep-sea fishes".

(9) Spiritualism

Unlike Conan Doyle, Faraday did not believe in spiritualism. Indeed he excoriated the spiritualists for their naivety of faith. In particular, Faraday wrote vehemently upon the subject of tilting and levitation of tables and chairs to Professor C. F. Schönbein, the discoverer of ozone, on 25th. July, 1853:

"I have not been at work except in turning the tables upon the table-turners, nor should I have done that, but that I thought it better to stop the inpouring flood by letting all know at once what my views and thoughts were. What a weak, credulous, incredulous, unbelieving, superstitious, bold, frightened, what a ridiculous world ours is, as far as concerns the mind of man. How full of inconsistencies, contradictions, and absurdities it is ...".

In a letter to *The Times* he wrote:

"I think the system of education that could leave the mental condition of the public body in the state in which this subject has found it, must have been greatly deficient in some very important principle".

Holmes, too, did not believe in the supernatural or legends such as those involving vampires. In *The Sussex Vampire*, he is quoted as saying:

"'Rubbish, Watson, rubbish! What have we to do with walking corpses who can only be held in their graves by stakes driven through their hearts? It's pure lunacy'".

Holmes further states in the same narrative:

"'This Agency stands flat-footed upon the ground, and there it must remain. This world is big enough for us. No ghosts need apply'".

Again, in *The Hound of the Baskervilles*, after having just heard the legend of the Hound, Holmes is asked if he finds it interesting, to which he replies that it is, but only "To a collector of fairy-tales".

(10) Religion

On this point there would seem to be a major difference between the two men. Faraday was, as already stated, a strict Sandemanian, believing in the literal truth of the Bible. Holmes, on the other hand, believed, in *The Naval Treaty*, that:

> "There is nothing in which deduction is so necessary as in religion. It can be built up as an exact science by the reasoner".

However, it would seem that, although a sceptic, he did have beliefs for, in *The Cardboard Box*, Holmes' states:

> "'What is the meaning of it, Watson?' said Holmes, solemnly, as he laid down the paper. 'What object is served by this circle of misery and violence and fear? It must tend to some end, or else our universe is ruled by chance, which is unthinkable. But what end? There is the great standing perennial problem to which human reason is as far from an answer as ever'".

(11) Politics

Faraday also had a healthy scepticism of politics and politicians as can be gathered from his response to the question as to what use his discoveries may be put. There is further evidence for his dislike of politics when in 1835 the Prime Minister, Viscount Melbourne, asked Faraday to call upon him since the Government wanted to give him a 'pension' to pursue work of public interest. At the meeting, Viscount Melbourne stated that the giving of such pensions was "humbug". Faraday, angered by this, left the meeting and later wrote declining the offer of money. The incident was reported in *The Times* and King William IV himself intervened, with the Prime Minister having to apologise to Faraday. Only after this did Faraday accept the 'pension' of three hundred pounds a year for life.

Faraday remarked to his friend, Auguste de la Rive, that "For me, who never meddle with politics and who think very little of them as one of the games of life, it seems sad that Scientific men should be so disturbed by them".

During the early association between Holmes and Watson, the latter came to believe that the former knew next to nothing of contemporary politics. In *A Study in Scarlet*, Watson lists the detective's knowledge on various subjects; politics is marked as being "feeble". Through his work (which included the case of "The Politician, the Lighthouse and the Trained Cormorant"), Holmes did come into contact with politicians, even the Prime Minister, but on the whole remained distanced from this sphere of interest, no doubt due to his scepticism of the subject and the people involved. This area was far more within the province of Mycroft Holmes, who, according to Sherlock in *The Bruce-Partington Plans*, occasionally **was** the British Government.

(12) Publications

Faraday had a compulsive urge to record all that he saw and thought. Apart from four hundred and fifty original papers he was also author of several books and monographs. The first was entitled *Chemical Manipulation* and was published in four volumes. Others included books based on his Christmas lectures, *Various Forces of Matter* in 1860, and the immensely popular *Chemical History of a Candle* the following year. He also wrote on the lecturer's art – giving advice to aspiring lecturers on continuity, diction and how to hold the interest of an audience. Most of those that may be considered monographs are works published in the *Proceedings of the Royal Institution*. These were on a diverse range of subjects and included not only scientific substance, but philosophical and poetic musings.

Holmes was also the author of a number of monographs. Each was on a technical subject and included a special study of tobacco ashes entitled *Upon the Distinction Between the Ashes of the Various Tobaccos*, the polyphonic motets of Lassus (which was printed for private circulation and said to be the last word upon the subject), a "trifling" monograph upon the subject of secret writings in which he analysed one hundred and sixty separate ciphers, another on the dating of documents, a further one on tattoos, and one upon the influence of the trade upon the hand. There were also a couple of articles about ears in *The Anthropological Journal* and the "somewhat ambitious" article entitled *The Book of Life* published in an English magazine in which he attempted to show how an observant man might learn by an accurate and systematic examination of all that came in his way. In retirement Holmes hoped to write a *Practical Handbook of Bee Culture*, and may well have intended writing those monographs he mentioned he would like to write in previous cases: upon the use of dogs in the work of the detective, malingering, and the typewriter in relation to crime. He also said he would devote his declining years to a textbook which would focus the whole art of detection into one volume.

(13) Maxims

Doubtless there are many quotations and maxims upon which both men would have agreed. To conclude this 'Baker Street' dozen I have chosen just one from each to illustrate that their minds were in accord with each other.

Faraday once said that he was "a very lively imaginative person" who "could believe in the *Arabian Nights* as easily as in the Encyclopaedia; but facts were important to me. I could trust a fact".

Facts were also important to Sherlock Holmes. In *A Study in Scarlet*, Holmes emphasises their importance by saying that "When a fact appears to be opposed to a long train of deductions, it invariably proves to be capable of bearing some other interpretation".

Bibliography

The Complete Sherlock Holmes, Sir Arthur Conan Doyle, Blitz Editions (undated).

The Encyclopaedia Sherlockiana, Jack Tracy, Avenue Books (1987).

The House of the Royal Institution, A. D. R. Caroe, Oliver Burridge & Co. (1963).

Michael Faraday and the Modern World, Brian Bowers, EPA Press (1991).

Michael Faraday and the Royal Institution (The Genius of Man and Place), John Meurig Thomas, IOP Publishing (1991).

Michael Faraday of the Royal Institution, Ronald King, The Royal Institution of Great Britain (1973).

The Sherlock Holmes Encyclopaedia, Matthew E. Bunson, Pavilion Books (1995).

Where Did Holmes Learn His Chemistry?

New Light On An Old Mystery

Doctor Antony J. Richards, M.R.I.

The very first time the reader learns of the existence of Sherlock Holmes in *A Study in Scarlet*, we are told that Holmes possesses a "profound" knowledge of chemistry. Holmes was certainly a most capable experimental chemist and it was entirely appropriate that the first meeting between Holmes and Watson took place in a chemical laboratory, where the former was investigating a reagent which he believed was precipitated by haemoglobin and nothing else – this being superior to the Guaiacum test which Holmes considered to be clumsy and uncertain. It is also most appropriate that Holmes, at the time of *The Final Problem*, tells Watson that he would be happy to devote more time to his chemical researches in his retirement.

The question remains: where did Holmes attain his chemical knowledge, and what inspired him to learn this difficult subject? Could it be that Holmes had a mentor? Could it be that the impetus came from the Royal Institution of Great Britain which, at that time, was the foremost chemical authority in the world? Indeed the purpose of the Royal Institution of Great Britain was:

"for diffusing and facilitating the general introduction of useful mechanical inventions and improvements and for teaching by courses of philosophical lectures and experiments, the applications of science to the common purposes of life".

Holmes once stated in *The Greek Interpreter* that he was descended from the French artist Vernet and that "art in the blood is liable to take the strangest forms". But surely science also runs in the blood and, following this line of thought, is it not entirely feasible that Holmes also had some scientific blood in his veins? Here, fortunately, the Royal Institution of Great Britain provides evidence to support this hypothesis in the form of Frederick Hale Holmes, who made joint researches with Professor Michael Faraday at the Institution in the early part of the nineteenth century. Unfortunately, little is known about this man, save his scientific achievements, but it cannot be coincidence that his researches allude to one of the great unchronicled cases mentioned in Watson's writings. Frederick Holmes, who is sometimes referred to as 'Professor' though of what and where it is not known, described himself in his patents as an analytical chemist of Blackwall and was still alive in the 1880s.

In 1836 there was a general reform of Trinity House, the body responsible for lighthouses around the British coast, undertaken by the Reform Parliament of the Whig Prime Ministers Charles, 2nd. Earl Grey and William Lamb, 2nd. Vicount Melbourne. As part of this programme of reform, the Deputy Master of Trinity House, John Henry

Pelly, decided that the Corporation needed to improve the light produced by its lighthouses and to thoroughly examine the various methods of doing so. Hence it was also in 1836 that Faraday was made a scientific advisor to Trinity House at an annual salary of two hundred pounds. Unfortunately, most of the papers relating to the work carried out by Faraday for Trinity House were destroyed during the Second World War, though one report to Parliament from 1860 does still survive and outlines the duties of the "commissioners appointed to enquire into the conditions and management of lights, buoys and beacons". In the report Faraday wrote:

"In 1836 I was appointed 'Scientific advisor to the Corporation of the Trinity House in experiments on Lights'. Since then a large part of my attention has been given to the lighthouses in respect of their ventilation, their lightning conductors and arrangements, the impurity and cure of water, the provision of domestic water, the examination of optical apparatus, etc., the results of which may be seen in various reports to Trinity House. A very large part also of my consideration has been given to the numerous propositions of all kinds which have been and are presented continually to the Corporation; few of these present any reasonable prospect of practical and useful application, and I have been obliged to use my judgement, chiefly in checking imperfect and unsafe propositions, rather than in forwarding any which could be advanced to a practical result."

One idea to improve the range of lighthouses was to use limelight. This involves a hydrogen flame burning in oxygen and heating a piece of lime to produce an intense light. Indeed the theory was sound and a brilliant white light is produced, but Faraday wondered whether the gases required could be produced reliably in the conditions of a lighthouse.

Another evaluation was performed on a system proposed by a Dr. Watson in 1852. Joseph John William Watson possessed a Ph.D. from an as yet unidentified university and is listed as a Fellow of the Geological Society from 1852 until 1888. Until 1858 he lived in England, first in London and then in Gloucestershire. From 1858 to 1872 he lived in Paris; thereafter his movements are unknown. Watson's system composed of, basically, passing an electric current from a battery across a carbon arc. Faraday rejected his work on three grounds: first that the light flickered too much, second that the fumes produced by the nitric acid battery were too great, and finally that the operation of the light would require more intelligent lighthouse keepers.

Much more promising, in Faraday's view, was the carbon arc produced by an electromagnetic machine driven by a steam engine, and in particular the arc lamp designed by Professor Holmes. Faraday hoped that the lamp could be tried:

> "... for a time and under circumstances during which all the liabilities may be thoroughly eliminated. The light is so intense, so abundant,

so concentrated and focal, so free from under shadow (caused in the common lamp by the burner), so free from flickering, that one cannot but desire that it should succeed".

The work done by Professor Frederick Holmes is outlined in a book entitled 'Holmes' Magneto-Electric Light, as applicable to Lighthouses'. The apparatus was first used near Dover at the South Foreland lighthouse (**Figure 1**) as the following extract shows:

"On the 8th. of December, 1858, a modification of that mysterious electric power, which – as applied to the mariner's compass – has piloted the sailor for centuries across the seas, was for the first time made to complete its friendly service of guidance and of warning, by being shown from a Lighthouse on the English coast. The Magneto-Electric Light was exhibited from the High Light at the South Foreland, near Dover, on that evening, and on those of several subsequent weeks".

It was an instant success as reported by the Royal Commissioners who, on the 29th. April 1859, stated that the light was:

"... far brighter than any other lights, visible either on the French or the English coast; that, at a distance of some miles, it threw a shadow, which could be seen clearly on the palm of the hand, and still more clearly on a white surface".

Figure 1 — The South Foreland lighthouse from a photograph taken by the author in 1997.

Holmes' book has an appendix in which are reports from various ships, each of which agreed that the new light was a great improvement on the traditional oil-lamps. Indeed, an experienced pilot on *H.M.S. Cossack* stated that the light could be seen for up to sixty miles. The commander of *S.S. Liverpool* confirmed the brilliance of the light even in haze.

The only reservation that Faraday had was the cost of building and operating the light. The actual factory cost was three thousand pounds for a pair of machines plus five hundred pounds for the lens and lantern. This compares to the lesser cost of just under three thousand pounds for a first-order dioptic oil-light apparatus. The running costs were predicted to be between six and seven hundred pounds per year as opposed to between three and five hundred pounds for the more traditional apparatus. However, it should be remembered that each lighthouse generated income from passing ships. In 1858 the combined income of the forty-seven lights under the Trinity House authority was two hundred and fifty-seven thousand pounds against an expenditure of just one hundred and seventy-two thousand pounds, which included thirty-eight thousand pounds for new building works. The extra cost of running the new lights was estimated to amount to only fourteen thousand one hundred pounds per year. This would seem a small price to pay for the obvious improvements.

The apparatus **(Figure 2)** was exhibited at the International Exhibition of 1862. The light was produced by bringing two carbon rods together to a fixed distance

Figure 2 –
Holmes' Magneto-Electric Light Apparatus as exhibited at the International Exhibition of 1862. (*Holmes' Magneto-Electric Light as applicable to Lighthouses,* Frederick Hale Holmes, 1861, publisher unknown)

and applying a strong electric field, thus forming an arc. The electric current was produced from the principle founded by Faraday in 1831 whereby:

"... a piece of soft iron, surrounded by a metallic wire, was passed by the poles of a magnet, an electric current was produced in the wire, which could be exalted so as to give a spark".

The apparatus was first demonstrated and described by Faraday in a discourse delivered on 9th. March, 1860:

"Many powerful magnets are ... arranged on a wheel, that they may be associated very near to another, on which are fixed many helices with their cores .... Again, a third wheel consists of magnets arranged like the first; next to this is another wheel of helices, and next to this again a fifth wheel carrying magnets. All the magnet-wheels are fixed to one axle, and all the helix wheels are held immoveable in their place. The wires of the helices are conjoined and connected with a commutator, which, as the magnet-wheels are moved round, gathers the various electric currents in the helices, and sends them up through two insulated wires in one common stream of electricity into the lighthouse lanthorn. So it will be seen that nothing more is required to produce the electricity than to revolve the magnet-wheels".

The large diameter of the electro-magnetic generator can clearly be seen in the illustration. One set of carbon rods is shown on the left side of the apparatus, while in practice these would be within the lens on the right. Note that the lens, manufacturered by Messrs. Chance, actually consists of four lenses (three of which are visible) on a rotating turntable. Although the lighthouse was said to be lit by electricity, the generator (and for that matter the lens rotation) was actually controlled by a steam engine located in a room below the main apparatus.

As carbon was consumed in the arcing process, a mechanism was required to ensure that the tips of the rods remained a fixed distance apart, that distance being judged to give the optimum illumination. This was achieved by the use of a second electro-magnet counterbalanced by a spring. The resulting separation was said to be accurate to one two-hundredth of an inch. Since each rod only lasted for approximately three and a half hours, two lamps were provided for each lens. These were on separate travelling platforms so that the lights could be replaced without interruption to the main light. It may sound a complex arrangement to the reader but Professor Holmes in his book described the working of the machinery as something:

"... any child could do."

Hence the theory that I should like to propose. First, that Professor Frederick Holmes was indeed a relation of Mr. Sherlock Holmes, possibly his father, but most certainly an influence upon the scientific development of Holmes.

Added to this, by noting the research interests of Frederick Holmes, it becomes clearer that this work was indeed related to the unchronicled case involving "the politician, the lighthouse and the trained cormorant" which hitherto has been attributed to Sherlock Holmes. The lighthouse in question is undoubtedly the South Foreland[1] where Professor Holmes' magneto-electric light apparatus was first installed, and the politician in question, I deduce, must have been either Charles, 2nd. Earl Grey, or William Lamb, 2nd. Viscount Melbourne. From the mention of the trained cormorant, one can surmise that the true nature of the appointment was not just to provide better lighting for the safe passage of vessels, but something more sinister.

The cormorant is a water bird of which there are approximately thirty species in two or three genera belonging to the family *Phalacrocoracidae.* Cormorants have little value to man and inhabit seacoasts, lakes and rivers, making their nests from seaweed and guano near cliffs or, more conventionally, from sticks in a bush or tree. They lay two to four chalky eggs, pale blue when fresh, which hatch in three to five weeks, with the young maturing in the third year. The most widespread cormorant is the common, or great, cormorant, *Phalacrocorax carbo.* This bird has a wing span of up to one hundred centimetres and is common from eastern

---

[1] Appendix B gives a short history of the South Foreland lighthouse from which it will be seen that the place was used for another experiment, which gives credence to the theory that it was very much linked to the covert operations of the British Government.

Canada to Iceland, across Eurasia to Australia and New Zealand, and in parts of Africa.

The most interesting fact about cormorants is that in the Orient, and elsewhere, these birds have been tamed and trained to dive for fish. It is not improbable then that the British Government of the time felt a need to train one, or more, cormorants for use at the South Foreland lighthouse — not for fishing, but the carrying of secret messages from British agents in Europe. The mere location of the South Foreland lighthouse, on the White Cliffs of Dover, is most indicative since it will be recalled that observers in Calais could clearly see the light.

Hence the lighthouse could be used to send coded messages to British agents in France, while the agents, who would not have the benefit of a magneto-electric light apparatus, could respond by sending a cormorant with a coded message attached in the normal way. The birds would have been trained to fly towards the bright light of South Foreland from where the messages could be dispatched to London with all due haste.

Further evidence that the light was used for more covert purposes is provided by the fact that, while under trial at South Foreland, the engineer and labourer who normally manned the lighthouse were replaced by one man who was "without previous instruction". Why was such a person chosen? It could only be because he had some other skill, such as telegraphy.

If further proof were needed one has only to read Professor Holmes' book in which he states that:

> "There are many functions connected with Lighthouses, which may be called secondary to the supreme purpose of showing the brightest and most constant light; but which are of sufficient importance to engage the attention of eminent scientific men, and for the satisfactory performance of which, every day brings an increasing demand".

One such secondary function was for shipping to be able to identify different lighthouses from their light, but as was revealed in the text, this function could easily be used for sending coded messages:

> "Again, besides flashing and revolving lights, this light, from the facility with which it can be instantly extinguished, and as instantly re-lighted to its full intensity – any number of times in quick succession – may be arranged to indicate a distinguishing number, repeated at intervals during the night".

More specifically:

> "... the Electric Light affords facilities for signalling, either for purposes of commerce or war ... either by day or night; the light being quite strong enough to be seen on the brightest day ..."

In this way the British Government could quicken its intelligence lines of communication with its agents in Europe in that there would now be no need for agents actually to cross the English Channel. This, I believe, was the true purpose of the work performed by Professor Frederick Hale Holmes.

Certainly Faraday took his work at South Foreland most seriously for there is a report of an elderly Faraday making a visit to the lighthouse in 1860:

"I went to Dover last Monday: was caught in a snow storm between Ashford and Dover and nearly blocked up in the train; could not go to the lighthouse that night; and finding the next day, that the roads on the downs were snowed up, returned to London: on Friday I again went down to Dover and proceeded by a fly that night, hoping to find the roads clear of snow: they were still blocked up towards the lighthouse, but by climbing over hedges, walls and fields (**Figure 3**), I succeeded in getting there and making the necessary inquiries and observations".

On his return Faraday was able to report:

"The light shone up and down the Channel, and across into France, with a power surpassing that of any other fixed light within sight, or any where existent. The experiment has been a good one".

Figure 3 – One of the fields an elderly Michael Faraday would have had to cross in order to reach the South Foreland lighthouse in the snows of February, 1860. This photograph, taken by the author in 1997, shows rather different weather conditions.

It must certainly have been something of great importance to induce Faraday, who did not usually travel far from his laboratory at the Royal Institution of Great Britain, to make such a journey. One can only speculate that some catastrophy must have beset the light which only Faraday could resolve. Indeed Faraday continued to monitor the performance of the light at the South Foreland in his late sixties and early seventies and in declining health.

In conclusion, I hope to have shed new light (no pun intended) upon one of the most famous unchronicled cases mentioned by Watson in the canon, as well as having found a new relative of Holmes who was responsible for Holmes' initial interest in science. It is certainly probable that Sherlock Holmes, as a young boy, made frequent visits to his academic relative at the Royal Institution of Great Britain. Here he may have been taught science, attended the Christmas lecture series held each year for a juvenile audience and become fascinated with his relative's work which no doubt the young Holmes would have realised was of national importance. Indeed this latter aspect may well have influenced the careers of both Sherlock Holmes and his elder brother to a lesser or greater extent.

Bibliography

Faraday in the Pits, Faraday at Sea, Frank A. J. L. James, in *Proceedings of the Royal Institution*, Volume 68, Oxford Science Publications, 277-301 (1997).

Holmes' Magneto-Electric Light as applicable to Lighthouses, Frederick H. Holmes (1861).

Michael Faraday and the Modern World, Brian Bowers, EPA Press (1991).

Michael Faraday and the Royal Institution (The Genius of Man and Place), John Meurig Thomas, IOP Publishing (1991).

Appendix A

Selected Royal Institution of Great Britain Discourses of a Holmesian Nature 1826 – 1997

Compiled by Doctor Antony J. Richards, M.R.I.

(a) Pre-Holmes

9-2-1827   Alfred Ainger
              The Principle of Security in Locks
              (Invaluable if planning a burglary.
              Holmes is known to have resorted to
              breaking and entering at least three times.
              The known cases are *The Retired
              Colourman*, *Charles Augustus Milverton*
              and *The Illustrious Client*.)

9-5-1828   Sir Charles Wheatstone
              On the Production of Sounds on a New
              Musical Instrument
              (Holmes was "an enthusiastic musician"
              as Watson states in *The Red-Headed
              League*.)

16-5-1828   John Knowles
             The Rise, Progress and Present State of
             Naval Architecture
             (Useful background information for *The
             Bruce-Partington Plans.*)

23-5-1828   William Brockendon
             A New Mode of Projecting Shot ‐ with
             Experimental Applications
             (General interest to Holmes.)

21-5-1830   Michael Faraday for Charles Wheatstone
             The Application of a New Principle in the
             Construction of Musical Instruments
             (Holmes, being a musician himself,
             would have had a general interest in this
             topic.)

13-5-1831   William Brockendon
             The Passage of the Alps by Hannibal
             (Might have been of interest since
             Holmes also crossed the Alps in *The
             Final Problem.*)

4-6-1832   Michael Faraday
             Morden's Machinery for Manufacturing
             Bramah's Locks
             (Useful information if going to burgle
             Charles Augustus Milverton. In this case
             Holmes stated that he had "always had an
             idea that I would have made a highly
             efficient criminal".)

10-4-1835   Dionysius Lardner
Notice of Halley's Comet
(Moriarty wrote on the "Dynamics of the Asteroid" as revealed in *The Valley of Fear.*)

22-4-1835   William Brockendon
Storms in the Alps in August 1834
(Good background information for the Swiss excursion in *The Final Problem.*)

1-5-1835   Dionysius Lardner
Halley's Comet
(The motion of comets should have appealed to Moriarty who wrote on the "Dynamics of the Asteroid".)

18-1-1839   Michael Faraday
On the Gymnotics of the Torpedo
(May have been part of *The Bruce-Partington Plans.*)

22-1-1847   Michael Faraday
Gun-Powder
(General interest to Holmes.)

28-5-1847 Charles Vincent Walker
The Electric Telegraph of the South Eastern Railway
(Might have given an indication of the distance between telegraph poles; a piece of information used by Holmes to impress Watson in *The Adventure of Silver Blaze*.)

21-1-1848 The Revd. William Whewell
The Use of Hypothesis in Science
(From *The Sign of Four* it is known that Holmes believed "a hypothesis nonetheless must cover all the facts".)

15-2-1850 The Revd. J. Barlow
A Bank of England Note
(Holmes came across many forgers and counterfeiters including one in *The Three Garridebs*.)

28-2-1851 Edward Cowper
On Lighthouses
(*The Veiled Lodger* included reference to "the politician, the lighthouse and the trained cormorant".)

9-5-1851   The Revd. Baden Powell
On the Recent Experiment Showing the
Rotation of the Earth by Means of the
Pendulum
(Watson relates that Holmes was ignorant
of the Copernican Theory in *A Study in
Scarlet.*)

26-3-1852   Edward Cowper
On the Principles of the Construction and
Security of Locks
(The last known burgling by Holmes was
in the *Illustrious Client.*)

22-4-1853   John Conolly
On the Past and Present Condition of the
Insane and the Characteristics of Insanity
(General interest to Holmes.)

(b) Pre-Holmes in London

17-2-1854   John Conolly
On the Characters of Insanity
(General interest to Holmes.)

4-5-1855   John Hall Gladstone
On Gunpowder and its Substitutes
(General interest to Holmes.)

9-5-1856   Henry Bradbury
                On the Security and Manufacture of Bank
                Notes
                (In both *The Three Garridebs* and *The
                Engineer's Thumb,* Holmes encountered
                counterfeiting operations.)

20-3-1857   John Watkins Brett
                Submarine Telegraph
                (May have been a specification in *The
                Bruce-Partington Plans.*)

19-2-1858   Sir Edward Beckett
                On Some of the Improvements in Locks
                Since the Great Exhibition of 1851
                ("Burglary has always been an alternative
                profession, had I cared to adopt it, and I
                have little doubt that I should have come
                to the front" stated Holmes in *The
                Retired Colourman.*   Accordingly the
                design of locks would have interested
                Holmes.)

4-2-1859   Sir Richard Owen
                On the Gorilla
                (At least Holmes knew it wasn't a gorilla
                at *Wistaria Lodge.*)

9-3-1860
    Michael Faraday
On Lighthouse Illumination - the Electric Light
(*The Veiled Lodger* included reference to "the politician, the lighthouse and the trained cormorant". A Professor Holmes also worked with Professor Faraday on lighthouse illumination. His contribution was mentioned in the discourse.)

23-3-1860
    Mervyn Herbert Nevil Strong-Maskelyne
On Diamonds
(Holmes was well acquainted with diamonds, including *The Mazarin Stone* and *The Blue Carbuncle.*)

31-1-1862
    William Hopkins
On the Motion of Glaciers
(General background information for Swiss travel in *The Final Problem.*)

30-1-1863
    Nicholas Patrick Stephen Wiseman
On the Points of Contact Between Science and Art
(In *The Greek Interpreter* Holmes stated that "art in the blood is liable to take the strangest forms".)

21-2-1865   Sir John Evans
On the Forgery of Antiquities
(Holmes came across many forgers,
including the Conk-Singleton forgery in
The Six Napoleons.)

19-2-1869   Charles Hanson Greville
On the Female Poisoners of the 16th. and
17th. Centuries
(Holmes remarked in *The Sign of Four*
that the most winning woman he ever
knew was hanged for poisoning three little
children for their insurance money.)

8-4-1870   The Rt. Hon. Thomas Henry Huxley
On the Pedigree of the Horse
(Holmes had a good knowledge of such
matters as demonstrated in *The
Adventure of Silver Blaze* and *Shoscombe
Old Place*.)

17-2-1871   Sir James Nicholas Douglass
On the Wolf Rock Lighthouse
(Could this be the lighthouse mentioned
in *The Veiled Lodger*?)

12-3-1871   Sir W. F. Drummond Jervois
On the Defence Policy of Great Britain
(Of probable interest to Mycroft and
Sherlock Holmes, especially since the

former may well have formulated the policy in the first instance.)

(c) Holmes in London

11-5-1877   Sir David Mackenzie Wallace
Secret Societies in Russia
(Holmes came across several Nihilists, including Professor Coram and his wife in the *Golden Pince-Nez.*)

13-2-1880   Sir William Henry Preece
The Telegraphic Achievements of Wheatstone
(General interest since this was Holmes' preferred method of communication.)

20-2-1880   The Revd. Hugh Reginald Hawels
Old Violins
(Interest to Holmes since he owned a Stradivarius as revealed in *The Cardboard Box.*)

21-5-1880   Franz Hueffer
Musical Criticism
(Being "an enthusiastic musician" Holmes would have had much to say on this topic.)

11-2-1881   Sir Robert Stawall Ball
The Distances of the Stars
(As author of the "Dynamics of the Asteroid" and having a general interest in

astronomy, Moriarty would have found this discourse of value.)

20-1-1882   Sir William Huggins
Comets
(General interest to Moriarty.)

5-5-1882   Robert Grant
The Proper Motions of the Stars
(General interest to Moriarty, but of more value to Holmes who in *A Study in Scarlet* confesses not to know of the Copernican theory.)

27-4-1883   Sir Charles William Siemens
Some of the Questions Involved in Solar Physics
(General interest to Moriarty, but also to Holmes who in *A Study in Scarlet* confesses not to know the composition of the Solar System.)

11-5-1883   The Rt. Hon. Thomas Henry Huxley
Oysters and the Oyster Question
(Almost certainly one for *The Dying Detective* who thinks oysters will overrun the world.)

7-3-1884   Sir Charles Vernon Boys
Bicycles and Tricycles in Theory and Practice
(Holmes was an expert on bicycle tyre types as revealed in the *Priory School*.)

23-4-1884   Sir David Gill
               Recent Researches on the Distances of the
               Fixed Stars and Some Future Problems in
               Sidereal Astronomy
               (General interest to Moriarty.)

11-6-1886   Sir James Dewar
               Recent Researches on Meteorites
               (Moriarty wrote on the "Dynamics of the
               Asteroid" and would have had an equal
               interest in meteorites.)

2-3-1888   Charles Meymott Tidy
               Poisons and Poisoning
               (Holmes was "well up" on poisons as
               Watson states in *A Study in Scarlet.*)

25-1-1889   Sir George Howard Darwin
               Meteorites and the History of Stellar
               Systems
               (In *A Study in Scarlet* it is revealed that
               Moriarty wrote on the "Dynamics of the
               Asteroid" which are physically related to
               meteorites.)

24-5-1889   The Revd. Stephen Joseph Perry
               The Solar Surface During the Last Ten
               Years
               (Holmes knew little of the composition of
               the Solar System as noted by Watson in *A
               Study in Scarlet.*)

31-1-1890   Sir Frederick Augustus Abel
             Smokeless Explosives
             (General interest to Holmes.)

28-2-1890   Sir Charles Hubert Hastings Parry
             Evolution in Music
             (Holmes "was an enthusiastic musician,
             being himself not only a very capable
             performer but a composer of no ordinary
             merit" as revealed in *The Red-Headed
             League*.)

30-5-1890   Andrew Ainslie Common
             Astronomical Telescopes
             (General interest to Moriarty.)

13-2-1891   Arthur Schuster
             Recent Total Solar Eclipses
             (General interest to Moriarty.)

27-2-1891   Percey Hetherington Fitzgerald
             The Art of Acting
             (In *The Sign of Four*, Athelney Jones tells
             Holmes that "you would have made an
             actor and a rare one".)

(d) The 'Great Hiatus'

29-5-1891   Sir David Gill
             An Astronomer's Work in a Modern
             Observatory
             (General interest to Moriarty.)

9-6-1893   Sir Thomas Edward Thorpe
The Recent Solar Eclipse
(General interest to Moriarty.)

(e) Holmes Returns to London

6-4-1894   Sir Victor Horsley
The Destructive Effects of Projectiles
(General interest to Holmes.)

25-5-1894   Sir Howard Grubb
The Development of the Astronomical Telescope
(General interest to Moriarty.)

1-2-1895   Sir Henry Irving
Acting: An Art
(Holmes "would have made an actor and a rare one" according to Athelney Jones in *The Sign of Four*.)

19-2-1897   George Johnstone Stoney
The Approaching Return of the Great Swarm of November Meteors
("Dynamics of the Asteroid" was the title of the book written by Moriarty who would have also been interested in meteors.)

22-4-1898   Sir William Henry Mahoney Christie
The Recent Eclipse
(General interest to Moriarty.)

23-3-1900   Sir Alexander Noble
             Some Modern Explosions
             (General interest to Holmes.)

25-5-1900   Sir Francis Fox
             The Great Alpine Tunnels
             (Holmes may have made use of these in
             The Final Problem.)

3-5-1901   Charles Mercier
             Memory
             (Holmes had immense knowledge in
             certain areas and by implication a
             superior memory as Watson notes in *A
             Study in Scarlet.*)

(f) Holmes in Retirement

5-6-1903   Herbert Hall Turner
             The New Star in Gemini
             (General interest to Moriarty.)

31-3-1905   Joseph Wright
             The Scientific Study of Dialects
             (General interest to Holmes who was a
             master of dialects.)

9-6-1905   Sir William Henry White
             Submarine Navigation
             (Might have been part of the original
             specification in *The Bruce-Partington
             Plans.*)

18-1-1907   Sir Alexander Noble
Fifty Years of Explosives
(General interest to Holmes.)

12-3-1909   Sidney George Brown
Modern Submarine Telegraphy
(Might have been included in *The Bruce-Partington Plans.*)

18-3-1910   Sir Joseph John Thomson
The Dynamics of a Golf Ball
(Makes a change from asteroids and may have given Moriarty an idea for a new book.)

26-1-1912   Bertram Hopkinson
The Pressure of a Blow
(Holmes investigated the pressure of a blow upon transfixing a pig with a barb-headed spear in *Black Peter.*)

24-4-1914   Sir Frank Watson
The Stars Around the North Pole
(General interest to Moriarty. Like the North Star Holmes once described Watson, in *His Last Bow,* as being the "one fixed point in a changing age".)

26-2-1915   The Revd. Aloysius Lawrence Cortie
Solar Eclipses of 1915
(General interest to Moriarty.)

9-3-1917   Sir Almroth E. Wright
                The Treatment of Wounds in War
                (Obvious interest to Dr. Watson who had
                been an army surgeon in Afghanistan as
                first mentioned in *A Study in Scarlet* and
                returned to his old service after *His Last
                Bow*.)

1-3-1918   Arthur George Green
                The Modern Dye-Stuff Industry
                (Holmes studied coal tar derivatives,
                which include dye-stuffs, during the 'Great
                Hiatus' as revealed in *The Empty
                House*.)

23-2-1923   Sir Arthur Stanley Eddington
                The Interior of a Star
                (General interest to Moriarty.)

11-4-1924   Sir Jocelyn Field Thorpe
                Colours, Stains and Dyes
                (Again of interest to Holmes who studied
                coal tar derivatives, which include dyes,
                whilst at Montpellier. He was also an
                expert on stains as revealed in *The Second
                Stain*.)

7-5-1926   Sir Frederick George Kenyon
English Illuminated Manuscripts
(Holmes exhibited great interest in early
English charters in *The Three Students*,
and deciphered the remains of the original
inscription upon a fifteenth century
palimpsest in *The Golden Pince-Nez*.)

13-5-1927   Sir Humphry Davy Rolleston
Concerning Old Age
(Even Holmes was worried about the
ageing process with respect to his mental
faculties, though time of course was always
constant at 1895.)

31-5-1935   Major Charles E. S. Phillips
The Characteristics of Violin Tone
(No doubt Holmes, being a violin player
himself, would have been able to
contribute his own thoughts to this topic.)

31-1-1936   C. E. K. Mees
Sensitising Dyes and Their Application
To Scientific Photography
(Although not interested in photography,
with the exception of one particular
picture, Holmes did study dyes, which are
derived from coal tar products, during the
'Great Hiatus'.)

20-11-1936   Herbert George Wells
World Encyclopaedia
(Holmes kept his own commonplace books which acted as his world encyclopaedia, while Jabez Wilson in *The Red-Headed League* copied out sections from 'Encyclopaedia Britannica'.)

14-6-1946   Captain W. W. Davies
Torpedoes, Their Use and Development During the War
(Might have been of relevance to *The Bruce Partington-Plans.*)

12-12-1947   H. Munro Fox
Red, Green and Blue Bloods
(In *A Study in Scarlet* Holmes claimed to have discovered a reagent which was precipitated by haemoglobin and nothing else.)

5-11-1948   C. G. Butler
Bee Behaviour
(Being a bee keeper and having written upon the subject, Holmes would have almost certainly been interested in this discourse.)

18-5-1949 A. L. Hetherington
     Chinese Ceramic Glazes
     (Baron Gruner, and to a lesser extent Dr.
     Watson, were experts upon Chinese
     pottery as revealed in *The Illustrious
     Client.*)

27-1-1950 Sir John Craig
     Past British Coinage
     (Holmes encountered counterfeiters of
     silver money in *The Engineer's Thumb*
     and *Shoscombe Old Place.*)

7-12-1951 Sir Harold Scott
     Our Police System – Its Development
     and Organisation
     (No doubt Holmes would have many
     thoughts on this subject.)

12-6-1953 A. E. Carey Foster
     The British Thoroughbred Horse
     (Holmes had direct dealings with
     racehorses in *The Adventure of Silver
     Blaze* and *Shoscombe Old Place*, while
     Dr. Watson's knowledge of such matters
     was paid for with about half of his wound
     pension.)

12-2-1954 C. Keith Simpson
     Science in Crime Detection
     (Holmes should probably have given this
     discourse!)

20-5-1955 Sir Wilfrid le Gros Clark
The Exposure of the Piltdown Forgery
(A fraud which has been linked, probably
wrongly, to Conan Doyle.)

31-1-1958 Sir William Lawrence Bragg
Gemstones
(Holmes came across gemstones in
several cases. Probably the most famous
are *The Blue Carbuncle* and *The
Mazarin Stone.*)

28-2-1958 Leon Radzinowicz
Changing Attitudes Towards Crime and
the Devices Used to Combat it
(Holmes would almost certainly have had
thoughts on this subject.)

10-6-1959 R. S. Nyholm
Colour in Inorganic Chemistry
(This would have been one of the topics
studied by Holmes in Montpellier during
the 'Great Hiatus' as revealed in *The
Empty House.*)

26-2-1960 Alexander Kennedy
The Scientific Lessons of Interrogation
(Holmes was a master of interrogation
and could certainly have contributed to
this discourse.)

22-2-1963   R. J. Harrison
             Bones, Teeth and Identification
             (Strangely Holmes made little use of such
             identification other than mention of "the
             upper condyle of a human femur" in
             Schoscombe Old Place.)

22-10-1965   B. D. Shaw
             Explosives
             (General interest to Holmes.)

28-2-1969   Charles A. Taylor
             Physics and Music
             (General interest to Holmes who was "an
             enthusiastic musician".)

5-11-1971   H. C. Longuet-Higgins
             Making Sense of Music
             (General interest to Holmes.)

18-2-1972   Yehudi Menuhin
             The Technique of Violin Playing
             (Undoubtedly of great interest to Holmes
             who, being a violin player, would have
             appreciated the advice of a master on the
             subject.)

3-11-1972   R. B. Cundall
             Explosives
             (General interest to Holmes.)

16-2-1979   Charles A. Taylor
               Science and the Violin Family
               (Again, being a violin player, this topic
               would have appealed to Holmes.)

24-10-1980   C. Keith Simpson
               Modern Methods of Crime Detection
               (Holmes would have had his own views
               on this subject which may well have
               differed from that of the police.)

19-11-1982   Eric A. Ash
               Pathological Science
               (Again this would have almost certainly
               been of interest to Holmes.)

22-5-1987   Malcolm S. Longair
               The Case of the Missing Fingerprints or
               Dr. Watson's Cosmology
               (General interest to Moriarty. Professor
               Longair took on the persona of Holmes
               during this Discourse which may have
               annoyed Moriarty if he had been able to
               be present.)

22-10-1993   Sir Graham Hills
Knowledge is Luggage: Travel Light
(Holmes certainly agreed with this
statement since in *The Five Orange Pips*
he says "a man should keep his little
brain-attic stocked with all the furniture
that he is likely to use, and the rest he can
put away in the lumber-room of his
library, where he can get it if he wants it".)

26-1-1996   Frank James
Faraday in the Pits, Faraday at Sea
(This discourse concentrated, in part, on
the research performed on lighthouse
illumination by Professor Holmes, in
conjunction with Faraday, at the
Institution.)

(g) Lectures Delivered by Holmes

17-2-1899   Sir Richard Rivington Holmes
George the Third as a Collector

14-3-1997   Richard Holmes
The Coleridge Experiment
(Interest to Holmes since the experiment
in question was performed by Humphry
Davy to try and cure Samuel Coleridge's
opium addiction.)

Bibliography

The Complete Sherlock Holmes, Sir Arthur Conan Doyle, Blitz Editions (undated).

Appendix B

South Foreland: More Than Just A Lighthouse

Doctor Antony J. Richards, M.R.I.

The white cliffs of South Foreland rise to an elevation of one hundred metres above the sea and overlook what is, perhaps, one of the most dangerous stretches of water around our coasts. It is not reefs of rock or isolated inlets that form the enemy to shipping, but vast stretches of sand in almost continuous shoals and banks from the estuaries of the Thames to the Humber. The most notorious of these sandbanks are the Goodwin Sands, extending for ten miles north to south and three miles east to west. The deep waters between these and the mainland are the famous Downs where vessels lie at anchor protected from easterly and westerly gales. The Goodwin Sands have been called the "Great ship swallower" and have claimed untold tons of shipping and the lives of many crewmen. A single storm in 1836 saw the loss of thirty vessels engulfed by the sands.

As early as 1634, the shipowners could stand the loss of life and cargo no longer and presented a petition for the building of a lighthouse on the South Foreland to provide some indication of the whereabouts of the sands. It must be remembered that lightships were not in common use until about 1795. Trinity House opposed the petition saying that in their opinion no lights were required on the Forelands and argued that the introduction of a toll would only be a "grievance to navigation". They further indicated that they would have built lighthouses if they had thought them necessary.

Charles I granted permission to Sir John Meldrum to erect two lighthouses (with fire beacons) to warn vessels against the dreaded Goodwin Sands. Under the patent, Sir John was also granted permission to build a further light at the North Foreland. The joint venture was for fifty years at an annual rent of twenty pounds. At South Foreland he built a high and a low light, the former being situated well back from the cliff edge and the latter some twenty-five metres from it. They were built of timber and plaster and in 1719 the lanterns were enclosed. The problem with this arrangement was that the lanterns would inevitably become blackened due to the smoke. Hence the light was poor and shipowners complained so bitterly that, in 1730, the lanterns were removed and the lights left as open coal fires. Such a fire would consume many tons of coal in a single night, while, in wet and stormy weather, it would be impossible to maintain a clear fire as the light would be shrouded in smoke. The keepers must have given a sigh of relief in 1793 when once again lanterns were enclosed and sperm-oil lamps fitted with reflectors installed. This arrangement also tended to soot up the glass of the lantern as observed by Robert Stevenson on his visit to the lighthouse in 1818. He described the apparatus as:

"... holding twelve to fourteen plated reflectors which were not thoroughly clean. The dwelling houses partake of that cleanliness which is so general in the cottages of the English".

The annual profit from the dues collected amounted to one thousand pounds. In 1843 the upper lighthouse was completely, rebuilt to the design of James Walker, 'Chief Engineer to Trinity House'. A castellated parapet and keeper's dwellings adjoin the tower. The lower lighthouse was also rebuilt in 1846 as an octagonal white stone tower. This too was designed by James Walker and the cost of the improvements together with the new dioptric lens and lamps was four thousand four hundred and nine pounds. The lights between them formed a leading light visible from the southern end of the Goodwin Sands.

What makes the lighthouse of particular interest is the number of experiments which were performed there between 1856 to 1899 and beyond. In December 1858 the strongest artificial light known at the time was tried out when Professor Holmes' magneto-electric lamp was installed and tested. It was not until January 1872 that oil was permanently abandoned in favour of electricity. Next the dynamo lighting system of Dr. Siemens was tried and considered more efficient. During 1884 and 1885 there were further experiments made to test coal gas as a source of illumination in preference to electricity. This method was not adopted. There were other tests performed to determine the relative efficiency of sirens and gunshots as fog signals.

Maybe the most important experiment associated with South Foreland was the first attempt to use radio communication as an aid to navigation. This was first tried on Christmas Eve of 1897. Marconi installed his equipment at the lighthouse and made contact with the East Goodwin Lightship some ten miles away. It is curious to note, if not suspicious, that the wireless was used in earnest to summon help when the steam ship *R. F. Mathews* of London ran down the East Goodwin Lightship on 28th. April 1899.

An extract from an address given on 7th. October 1898 by the Chairman of the Wireless Telegraph and Signal Company (later to become Marconi's Wireless Telegraph Co. Ltd.) outlines the importance of this experiment:

"In December of last year the Company thought it desirable to demonstrate that the system was available for telegraphic communication between lightships and the shore.

This, as you are aware, is a matter of much importance, as all other systems tried so far have failed. The cables are exceedingly expensive, and require special moorings and fittings, which are troublesome to maintain and liable to break in storms. The officials of Trinity House offered us the opportunity of demonstrating to them the utility of the system between the South Foreland Lighthouse and one of the following light-vessels − viz. the Gull, the South Goodwin, and the East Goodwin. We naturally chose the one farthest away — the East Goodwin — which is just twelve miles from the South Foreland Lighthouse.

The apparatus was taken on board in an open boat and rigged up in one afternoon. The installation started working from the very first, 24th. December, without the slightest difficulty. The system has continued to work admirably through all the storms, which during this year have been remarkable for their continuance and severity. On one occasion, during a big gale in January last, a very heavy sea struck the ship, carrying part of her bulwarks away. The report of this mishap was promptly telegraphed to the Superintendent of Trinity House, with all details of the damage sustained.

The height of the wire on board the ship is eighty feet the mast being sixty feet of its length of iron, and the remainder of wood. The aerial wire is lead down a great number of metal stays and chains, which do not appear to have any detrimental effect on the strength of the signals.

The instruments are placed in the aft cabin, and the aerial wire comes through the framework of a skylight, from which it is insulated by means of a rubber pipe. As usual, a ten inch coil is used, worked by a battery of dry cells, the current taken being about six to eight amperes at fourteen volts.

Various members of the crew learned in two days how to send and receive, and, in fact, how to run the station; and owing to the Assistant on board not being as good a sailor as the instruments have proved to be, nearly all the messages during very bad weather are sent and received by these men, who previous to our visit to the ship, had probably never heard of wireless telegraphy, and were certainly unacquainted with even the rudiments of electricity. It is remarkable that wireless telegraphy, which has been considered by some as rather uncertain, or that might work one day and not the next, has proved in this case to be more reliable, even under such unfavourable conditions, than the ordinary land wires, very many of which were broken down in the storms of last month.

The instruments at the South Foreland Lighthouse are similar to those on the ship; but as we contemplate making some long distance tests from the South Foreland to the coast of France, the height of the pole is much greater than would be necessary for the lightship installation alone".

The world did not have to wait long before tests were made to communicate by wireless between England and France over a distance of twenty-eight miles. The following is a report from the *Daily Graphic* on 30th. March 1899:

"On this side of the Channel the operations took place, by permission of the Trinity House, in a little room in the front of the engine house from which the power is derived for the South Foreland Lighthouses. The house is on top of the cliff overlooking the Channel. The demonstrations are being conducted for the benefit of the French Government, who have the system under observation, and besides Signor Marconi there were present at the Foreland yesterday Colonel Comte du Bontavice de Heussey, French Military Attaché in England; Captain Ferrie, representing the French Government; and Captain Fieron, French Naval Attaché in England. During the afternoon a great number of messages in French and English crossed and recrossed between the little room at the South Foreland and the Chalet d'Artois, at Wimereux, near Boulogne.

The whole apparatus stood upon a small table about three foot square in the centre of the room. Underneath the table the space was fitted with about fifty primary cells; a ten inch induction coil occupied the centre of the table. The spark is one centimetre in length or about three quarters of an inch; the pole off the top of which the current went into space is one hundred and fifty feet in height. The length of the spark and power of the current were the same as used for communication with the East Goodwin Lightship, a fact that seems remarkable when it is considered that the distance over which the messages were sent yesterday was nearly three times as great. The greater distance is compensated for by the increased height of the pole.

Throughout the whole of the messages sent yesterday there was not once a fault to be detected – everything was clearly and easily recorded. The rate of transmission was about fifteen words a minute".

The 'Admiralty List of Lights' for 1903 described the South Foreland as having two fixed electric bright lights shining from white towers, sixty-nine feet and forty-nine feet in height set in line North eighty-five west, three hundred and eighty-five yards apart. They formed a leading light seen clearly from the South end of the Goodwin Sands. Soon afterwards the lower tower was discontinued due to cliff erosion. The upper white castellated tower, which was left standing, was modernised in 1969 and electrified from the mains grid (with a standby generator). It produced one million candle power and was visible for up to twenty six-miles giving a characteristic white group flashing three times every twenty seconds. There was no fog horn at the station, which was automated in 1959. The lighthouse was decommissioned on 30th. September 1988 and in 1989 was acquired by the National Trust. Today this unique landmark on top of the White Cliffs of Dover is preserved for the nation and is open to the public as a reminder of Britain's maritime history.

All this may indicate to the Holmesian that the South Foreland had duties other than to warn ships of the

Goodwin Sands. It certainly does not need a great imagination to propose that the various experiments performed here could have had other uses which Professor Holmes was involved in implementing initially, and Mycroft Holmes would certainly have known about. Certainly the presence of military personnel at the South Foreland during the wireless experiments of March 1899 indicated that both the French and British Governments regarded these developments of some importance. It would also seem that there was at this time some collaboration between the respective countries. It could even be proposed that the R. F. Mathews incident was no accident and that maybe it was an attempt by another power to disrupt radio signalling between the South Foreland and British or French Government agents in France. It is probable that they mistakenly thought that the lightship acted as a relay station since the radio signal was not powerful enough to traverse the whole of the English Channel.

This theory may, or may not, be true, but which ever way one regards the lighthouse at South Foreland it was certainly *more than just a lighthouse.*

Bibliography

South Foreland Lighthouse, document S(PR)2 39, Trinity House Lighthouse Service, Tower Hill, London, United Kingdom (undated).

South Foreland Lighthouse, information sheet published by the National Trust for Kent and East Sussex region, Lamberhurst, Kent, United Kingdom (undated).

It is hoped that on reading this book you may be moved to find out more about the various societies and institutions mentioned herein. Below are some contact details which may be of use for those seeking to continue their Holmesian and scientific studies.

Institute of Physics
76 Portland Place, London W1N 3DH
http://www.iop.org

Irregular Special Railway Company
170 Woodland Road, Sawston, Cambridge CB2 4DX.
http://mesdec3.me.ic.ac.uk/sherlock

National Trust
Kent & East Sussex Regional Office, Scotney Castle, Lamberhurst, Tunbridge Wells, Kent TN3 8JN

Royal Institution of Great Britain
21 Albemarle Street, London W1X 4BS.
http://www.ri.ac.uk

Royal Society of Chemistry
Library and Information Centre, Burlington House, Piccadilly, London W1V 0BN.
http://chemistry.rsc.org

Sherlock Holmes Society of London
Correspondence Secretary, 3 Outram Road, Southsea, Hampshire PO5 1QP.

Society of Chemical Industry
14/15 Belgrave Square, London SW1X 8PS.
http://sci.mond.org

Trinity House Lighthouse Service
Trinity House, Tower Hill, London EC3N 4DH.